The Way to Pass

Maths

3

GCSE
Intermediate Level

The Way to Pass
National Curriculum
Maths

GCSE
Intermediate Level

Arnold Burdett

VERMILION
LONDON

First published in 1994

3 5 7 9 10 8 6 4 2

Text copyright © Rockhopper 1994

First published in the United Kingdom in 1994
by Vermilion
an imprint of Ebury Press
Random House, 20 Vauxhall Bridge Road,
London SW1V 2SA

Random House Australia (Pty) Limited
20 Alfred Street, Milsons Point, Sydney,
New South Wales 2061, Australia

Random House New Zealand Limited
18 Poland Road, Glenfield,
Auckland 10, New Zealand

Random House South Africa (Pty) Limited
PO Box 337, Bergvlei, South Africa

Random House UK Limited Reg. No. 954009

Editor: Alison Wormleighton
Design: Jerry Goldie Graphic Design

A CIP catalogue record for this book
is available from the British Library

ISBN 0-09-178121-3

Typeset by AFS Image Setters Ltd, Glasgow
Printed in Great Britain by Butler & Tanner Ltd,
London and Frome

Foreword

Welcome to THE WAY TO PASS MATHS GCSE INTERMEDIATE LEVEL. I want to tell you why I have put together this series of books, along with a team of teachers, advisers and examiners.

A lot of people don't enjoy Maths because they're frightened of it. I can understand how frightening it can be because I've been scared of it myself at times: maybe the teacher goes through the work a little too quickly for you, maybe there are too many children in your class, maybe you're not the best at Maths in your class. All of these reasons can make Maths seem impossible. What I have learned through the years is that the more help you have and the longer you spend on something, the more likely you are to get over any difficulties.

If you're studying for GCSE Maths Intermediate Level, then you will already know that you may be able to achieve as high as a B grade, and it is well worth trying for. Whatever you might think about school, and about Maths in particular, there is no doubt that Maths and English are the two most important subjects for you to do well in. If you understand most of what you're taught, you are set for a brighter future, being able to do some of the things you've always wanted to. THE WAY TO PASS can help you through your GCSE course, making the subjects you're taught a little more understandable and interesting, making your exams easier and helping you to get the best grades possible.

All of the books are based around work for you to do at home. Most of the explanations will have been covered in classes at school and so you won't want to wade through pages and pages of more explanations. That is why in each section we give you a concise list of the main things you need to know, and then work through exercises to practise each one.

This completely new range of books has been organised so that, if you want to, you can follow the already successful VIDEO CLASS videos covering the same subjects/levels. All of the book sections work together neatly with the video sections so that you have a complete course at your fingertips. Alternatively, the books can be used on their own, without the videos.

I certainly hope that this series will make Maths and English more approachable and slightly friendlier than they were before. Remember, you must follow what is taught in school and do as many exercises as you can – the more practice you get, the better you will be.

Carol Vorderman

Contents

The National Curriculum

The National Curriculum sets targets for pupils of all abilities from age 5 to 16, specifying what they should know, understand and be able to do at each stage of their education. It is divided into four **Key Stages**: Key Stage 1 (age 5–7), Key Stage 2 (age 7–11), Key Stage 3 (age 11–14) and Key Stage 4 (age 14–16).

At the end of Key Stages 1, 2 and 3, pupils take national tests in the **core subjects**: Maths and English (at age 7, 11 and 14) and Science (at age 11 and 14). At the end of Key Stage 4 (age 16) the **GCSE examinations** are the main way of assessing children's progress.

Whereas in the tests at Key Stages 1, 2 and 3 children achieve particular **Levels**, moving up one Level every two years or so, in the GCSE examination they are graded from A (at the top) to G (at the lower end of the scale). The grade A* may be awarded for exceptional achievement. U stands for ungraded or unclassified.

Nearly all pupils take GCSE examinations in English and in Maths. There are different **tiers** of paper to suit the varying capabilities of the pupils, and the grading system reflects the difficulty of the papers taken. Teachers decide which level is best suited to each pupil, who then has a clearly defined target to aim for.

THE WAY TO PASS books are all based on National Curriculum requirements. The GCSE English book covers the main elements of the syllabus at each tier, while GCSE Maths is split into three different books – Foundation, Intermediate and Higher – corresponding to the three tiers of the examination papers. The books will serve as a valuable back-up to a child's classwork and homework and provide an excellent preparation for the GCSE examinations.

Introduction

When you are studying for GCSE examinations, you are often looking for that extra bit of help. The WAY TO PASS series is designed to help you learn the facts and put them into practice, revising at your own pace and concentrating on the areas you need to work on most. This book is aimed at Intermediate Level (also sometimes known as Central Tier or 'Q' Level), which covers grades B–E.

Revision should not be rushed. Try to devise a revision timetable, spending about a week on one or two sections. First, check that you know all the facts set out under **Things You Need to Know** in each section. Next, work through the **How to Do It** exercises, which are worked examples showing you how to answer each type of question relating to that section. Cover each solution as you do it, then check to see you have answered it correctly. When you feel confident that you have understood the work in that section, try the **Do It Yourself** exercises. You'll find the **Answers** near the end of the book.

The numbering system used in the book makes it easy for you to concentrate on whatever topics you feel you most need to revise. Each topic within a section has a number, which identifies that topic throughout the section. Thus, in Section 1, for example, an explanation of Standard Form appears in no. 8 of Things You Need to Know; then exercises 8a, 8b and 8c of How to Do It show you how to answer questions involving Standard Form; and finally you can check how well you understand Standard Form with Do It Yourself exercises 8a, 8b and 8c.

You do not have to work through the book in any particular order; indeed, you should spend more time revising topics you are not very good at. However, sections 2, 7, 11 and 16 – the sections on number patterns, the metric system, angles and algebra – are particularly important if you are aiming at grade B level.

About a week before the examination, you can attempt the **Sample Exam Paper** at the end of the book. It is made up of the type of questions you will get in the actual exam, and should take you about one-and-a-half to two hours to do. You can check your solutions with those at the back of the book. If it were a real GCSE exam, you'd need to get about 75 per cent correct for grade C level, and about 85 per cent correct for grade B level. If there are topics you are still weak in, go back and look at these before the exam.

In the actual examination, do not spend too long on any one question. You can always go back if you have time at the end. Make sure that your solutions are easy to follow and neatly written out. Do not leave out essential working. You will lose marks if a question asks you to show your working and you give only the answer.

Try to enjoy your revision. You'll be surprised how this helps. Don't leave it to the last minute before your exam. Remember, the more you practise, the better you will cope.

1

Number Work and Indices

Things You Need to Know

1 **Rounding** – to round to a particular number of **decimal places** (d.p.) count the required number of figures from the decimal point and look at the figure after the last required place. If it is 5 or higher then the last figure is increased by 1, otherwise it is left as it is. For example:

> 4.794 is 4.8 to one decimal place and 4.79 to two decimal places

Numbers sometimes need to be corrected to a particular number of **significant figures** (s.f.). To count the significant figures in a number, count the number of digits, but in a figure less than 1, don't count the zeros between the decimal point and the first non-zero digit. Nor should you count the 'trailing' zeros at the end of a number. You *should*, however, count the zeros between digits.

To correct to a particular number of significant figures, do the same as for decimal places but correct from the *left*. Don't forget to put zeros for the digits you are rounding off, as they keep place value.

Sometimes the zero may be significant. Here is an example where the zero can be a significant figure:

> 7599 is 7600 correct to three significant figures
> or is 7600 correct to two significant figures

You may be asked to round to the nearest ten, hundred, thousand, and so on. This is similar to the other forms of rounding. To round to the nearest *ten*, look at the unit digit. If it is below 5, you round down; if it is 5 or above, you round up. Similarly, to round to the nearest *hundred*, look at the tens digit and follow the same rule. To round to the nearest *thousand*, look at the hundreds digit and follow the rule; and so on.

> 87 245.6 is 87 246 to the nearest whole one
> 87 250 to the nearest ten
> 87 200 to the nearest hundred
> 87 000 to the nearest thousand

2 **Factors** – the factors of a number are those numbers that divide exactly into the number. For example:

> The factors of 20 are   1   2   4   5   10 and 20
> The factors of 36 are   1   2   3   4   6   9   12   18 and 36

Common factors are factors of both numbers. For example:

> The common factors of 20 and 36 are   2 and 4

(The number 1 is not normally given as a common factor.)
   Prime factors are those factors which have no factors other than 1 and themselves. For example:

> The prime factors of 36 are 2 and 3

(The number 1 is not normally regarded as prime.) It is possible to express a number in terms of its prime factors. For example:

$$36 = 12 \times 3$$
$$= 2 \times 6 \times 3$$
$$= 2 \times 2 \times 3 \times 3$$
$$= 2^2 \times 3^2$$

$$20 = 4 \times 5$$
$$= 2 \times 2 \times 5$$
$$= 2^2 \times 5$$

3 **Prime numbers** are those numbers that have no factors other than 1 and the number itself. The number 1 is not normally classed as a prime number and 2 is the only even prime number (all the other even numbers have 2 as a factor). For example:

> The first five prime numbers are   2   3   5   7   11

'With significant figures, we don't count the 0 when it is a leading 0 or usually when it is a trailing 0 – it is counted when it is in the middle of other figures'

4 **Multiples** – the multiples of a number are those numbers that can be divided by the original number. For example:

Some multiples of 3 are   3   6   9   33   90   180   300   360

5 **Reciprocals** – the reciprocal of a number is the result of dividing the number into 1. For example:

The reciprocal of 5 is $1 \div 5$ which is $\frac{1}{5}$
The reciprocal of $\frac{1}{3}$ is $1 \div \frac{1}{3}$ which is 3

6 **Negative numbers** refer to a position below (or to the left of) some zero point. When two signs come together like: $2 + (-3)$ consider how the signs affect each other and the outcome. This is summarised as:

1st sign	2nd sign	Result
+	+	+
+	−	−
−	+	−
−	−	+

So $2 + (-3)$ becomes $2 - 3$, which is -1.

The same rules apply when we multiply two numbers together. For example:

$-3 \times -6 = +18$ (we would not normally put the '+' sign in)

7 **Index numbers** or **powers** are a way of saying how many times a number is multiplied by itself. For example, in

$$7 \times 7 \times 7 \times 7 \times 7 \times 7 \times 7 \times 7 \times 7 = 7^9$$

the '9' tells how many of the '7s' have been multiplied together. The rules for handling this shorthand are fairly straightforward (providing the base number is the same).

$$n^a \times n^b = n^{a+b}$$
$$n^a \div n^b = \frac{n^a}{n^b} = n^{a-b}$$
$$(n^a)^b = n^{a \times b}$$

A negative power means '1 over'. For instance:

$$2^{-2} = \frac{1}{2^2} = \frac{1}{4}$$

There is one special power and that is 0. Whatever the number to the power of 0 the result is 1 – here is one reason why we consider it to be 1:

$$12^0 \times 12^7 = 12^{0+7} = 12^7$$

So 12^0 has not changed 12^7.

We call the power of 2 the **square** of the number and the power of 3 the **cube** of the number. For example:

The square of 7 means 7^2 which is 49.
The cube of 5 means 5^3 which is 125.

The reverse of squaring is finding the **square root** – i.e. what number when squared gives that number. Similarly, the **cube root** is the number which when cubed gives that number. The sign

$$\sqrt{}$$

is used for square roots and the sign

$$\sqrt[3]{}$$

is used for cube roots. For example:

$$\sqrt{81} = 9$$
$$\sqrt[3]{216} = 6$$

It is very useful to know the squares of at least the numbers 1 to 10, which means you'll also know the square roots of those squares.

8 When numbers are very large, like the speed of light (299 500 km/second, or 1 078 200 000 km/hour) or very small, like the mass of the electron

0.000 000 000 000 000 000 000 000 000 910 929

it is easier to write them down in **standard form** with the decimal place so that the number is between 1 and 10. The number has to be multiplied by a power of 10 to reposition the decimal point in the correct place. Counting how many figures the decimal point has been moved tells you what power of 10 has been used. (A minus sign indicates the original number was less than 1.) For example:

$$299\,500 = 2.995 \times 10^5$$

$$0.000\,000\,000\,000\,000\,000\,000\,000\,000\,910\,929 = 9.109\,29 \times 10^{-28}$$

How to Do It

'When a calculator gives answers with many figures after the decimal point, we usually need to round the answer'

1 Use a calculator to find the value of each of the following. Correct your answer to the accuracy asked for.

  (i) 3.24×2.69 (3 d.p.)   (ii) $6.472 \div 0.783$ (2 d.p.)
  (iii) 56.8×27.75 (to nearest 10)   (iv) 12.456×3.58 (4 s.f.)

Solution

  (i) $3.24 \times 2.69 = 8.7156$ (on a calculator)
             $= 8.716$ (3 d.p.)
  (ii) $6.472 \div 0.783 = 8.265\,645$ (on a calculator)
                  $= 8.27$ (2 d.p.)
  (iii) $56.8 \times 27.75 = 1576.2$ (on a calculator)
                  $= 1580$ (to nearest 10)
  (iv) $12.456 \times 3.58 = 44.592\,48$ (on a calculator)
                  $= 44.59$ (4 s.f.)

2 Find the factors of the numbers 24, 42 and 75. What factors do all three numbers have in common?

Solution

The factors of 24 are   1   2   3   4   6   8   12   24
The factors of 42 are   1   2   3   6   7   14   21   42
The factors of 75 are   1   3   5   15   25   75

They have only 1 and 3 in common.

3 List all prime numbers less than 100 which are greater than 60.

Solution

61   67   71   73   79   83   89   97

4 State the multiples of 14 and 35 which are less than 150. What is the lowest multiple they have in common?

Solution

The multiples of 14 are   14   28   42   56   70   84   98   112   126   140
The multiples of 35 are   35   70   105   140

The lowest common multiple of 14 and 35 is 70.

5 Find the value of the reciprocal of:

(i) 0.85   (ii) 2.5   (iii) the reciprocal of 7

Where necessary correct your answer to 3 s.f.

Solution

(i) Using a calculator the reciprocal of 0.85 is $1.176\,4706 = 1.18$ (3 s.f.).
(ii) Using a calculator the reciprocal of 2.5 is 0.4.
(iii) Using a calculator the reciprocal of the reciprocal of 7 is the reciprocal of $0.142\,8571 = 7$.

'You don't really need to use a calculator for the third one!'

6a The diagram shows a thermometer scale in degrees Celsius. What are the temperatures labelled X and Y? What is the difference in temperature between X and Y?

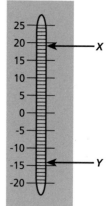

Solution
X is 19 °C and Y is -14 °C. The difference is 33 °C.

b In Greece the clocks are 2 hours ahead of London time, while California is 8 hours behind. If you fly from California to Greece, by how much do you alter your watch?

Solution
Answer = 10 hours forward. (As you fly from California you must alter your watch forward by 8 hours to adjust to London time and then a further 2 hours to adjust to Greek time.)

c Evaluate the following:

$$\text{(i)} \;\; -4 \times 3 \qquad \text{(ii)} \;\; -5 \times -7 \qquad \text{(iii)} \;\; -48 \div 12$$
$$\text{(iv)} \;\; -1 \times -2 \times -3 \times -4 \times -5$$

Solution

(i) $-4 \times 3 = -12$
(ii) $-5 \times -7 = +35$ (or just 35)
(iii) $-48 \div 12 = -4$
(iv) $-1 \times -2 \times -3 \times -4 \times -5 = -120$ (take care with the signs!)

7a Simplify the following:

$$\text{(i)} \;\; 4^2 \times 4^5 \qquad \text{(ii)} \;\; 5^7 \times 5^{-3} \qquad \text{(iii)} \;\; 4^5 \div 4^{-2} \qquad \text{(iv)} \;\; (\tfrac{1}{2})^3 \div (\tfrac{1}{2})^{-6}$$

Solution

(i) $4^2 \times 4^5 = 4^{2+5} = 4^7$
(ii) $5^7 \times 5^{-3} = 5^{7+(-3)} = 5^4$
(iii) $4^5 \div 4^{-2} = 4^{5-(-2)} = 4^{5+2} = 4^7$
(iv) $(\tfrac{1}{2})^3 \div (\tfrac{1}{2})^{-6} = (\tfrac{1}{2})^{3-(-6)} = (\tfrac{1}{2})^9$

(Since $\tfrac{1}{2}$ is 2^{-1}, we could write it as 2^{-9}, but normally it would be left as shown above.)

b What is $\dfrac{3^9}{3^6 \times 3^5}$ as a single power of 3?

Solution

$$\frac{3^9}{3^6 \times 3^5} = \frac{3^9}{3^{6+5}} = \frac{3^9}{3^{11}} = 3^{9-11} = 3^{-2}$$

c Replace the ? by the correct index value.

(i) $9 = 3^?$ (ii) $2^? = 16$ (iii) $100\,000 = 10^?$ (iv) $\frac{1}{4} = 2^?$

Solution

(i) $9 = 3^?$ $? = 2$ $(9 = 3^2)$
(ii) $2^? = 16$ $? = 4$ $(2^4 = 16)$
(iii) $100\,000 = 10^?$ $? = 5$ $(100\,000 = 10^5)$
(iv) $\frac{1}{4} = 2^?$ $? = -2$ $(\frac{1}{4} = 2^{-2})$

8

a Convert the following to standard form:

(i) $57\,000$ (ii) $0.000\,69$ (iii) 34×10^3 (iv) 0.64×10^{-7}

Solution

(i) $57\,000 = 5.7 \times 10^4$ (ii) $0.000\,69 = 6.9 \times 10^{-4}$
(iii) $34 \times 10^3 = 3.4 \times 10 \times 10^3$ (iv) $0.64 \times 10^{-7} = 6.4 \times 10^{-1} \times 10^{-7}$
$\qquad\qquad\quad = 3.4 \times 10^4$ $\qquad\qquad\qquad = 6.4 \times 10^{-8}$

b What are the following in ordinary notation?

(i) 3.5×10^4 (ii) 2.9×10^{-5} (iii) $5.983\,67 \times 10^3$

Solution

(i) $3.5 \times 10^4 = 35\,000$
(ii) $2.9 \times 10^{-5} = 0.000\,029$
(iii) $5.983\,67 \times 10^3 = 5983.67$

c Work out the following, leaving your answer in standard form:

(i) $(1.8 \times 10^3)^2$ (ii) $(4 \times 10^8)^3$ (iii) $(5.1 \times 10^{-6})^3$

Solution

(i) $(1.8 \times 10^3)^2 = 1.8 \times 10^3 \times 1.8 \times 10^3$
$= 3.24 \times 10^6$

(ii) $(4 \times 10^8)^3 = 4 \times 10^8 \times 4 \times 10^8 \times 4 \times 10^8$
$= 4^3 \times (10^8)^3$
$= 64 \times 10^{24}$
$= 6.4 \times 10^{25}$

(iii) $(5.1 \times 10^{-6})^3 = 5.1 \times 10^{-6} \times 5.1 \times 10^{-6} \times 5.1 \times 10^{-6}$
$= 5.1^3 \times (10^{-6})^3$
$= 132.651 \times 10^{-18}$
$= 1.32651 \times 10^2 \times 10^{-18}$
$= 1.32651 \times 10^{-16}$

Do It Yourself

1
a Write each of the following numbers in three ways:

correct to the nearest 100;
correct to three significant figures;
correct to two decimal places:

(i) 9326.686   (ii) 85.513   (iii) 227.245

b Using a calculator find the following and write your answers correct to three significant figures:

(i) $\sqrt{7}$ (ii) $2\sqrt{11}$ (iii) $\dfrac{5}{9}$ (iv) 3.412^2

2 On a copy of the diagram at the side put in their correct places the factors of 12, the factors of 42 and the factors of 54.

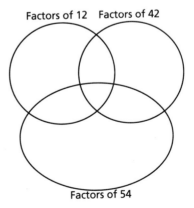

Factors of 12   Factors of 42

Factors of 54

3 Write down all the prime numbers which are greater than 100 and less than 150.

4 Write down the multiples of 7, the multiples of 11 and the multiples of 3 which are in the set of numbers:

     18 25 33 42 51 66 70 77 84 91 96

One of the numbers has not been chosen; which is it?

5 a Using a calculator find the reciprocal of:

    (i) 3.141 59   (ii) 6   (iii) 0.125   (iv) $\frac{3}{4}$ (v) 0.333 333 333 33 . . .

  b If R(5) means find the reciprocal of 5, find:

    (i) R(2) + R(4)   (ii) R($\frac{1}{2}$) + R(4)   (iii) R(R(8) + R(5))

6 Work out (or evaluate):

    (i) $-11 + 7$ (ii) $-8 + (-6)$ (iii) $7 - (-2)$ (iv) $\dfrac{6}{-3}$

    (v) $(-4) \times (-7)$ (vi) $-21 \div 3$ (vii) $5(3 - (-7))$ (viii) $\dfrac{7 \times (-6)}{-3}$

    (ix) $(-6) \times (-4) \times (-10)$ (x) $\dfrac{6 \times (-2) - 3}{-4}$

7 Simplify:

    (i) $2^2 \times 2^3$ (ii) $4^3 \times 4^4$ (iii) $3^6 \div 3^4$ (iv) $2^8 \div 2^2$

8 a Write the following numbers in standard form:

    (i) 5971   (ii) 78 000   (iii) 0.003 52   (iv) 14 million

  b (i) If 310 000 $= 3.1 \times 10^n$, what is the value of n?
    (ii) What is 4.1×10^{-3} as a decimal?

  c Work out:

    (i) $(6 \times 10^{-3}) \div (4 \times 10^{-1})$ (ii) $(3 \times 10^{-4}) \times (4 \times 10^6)$

2

Number Patterns

Things You Need to Know

1 **Triangular numbers** are those where the number of objects can be set out in a triangular shape – the first (or top) row is one object, the second row is two objects, the third row is three objects and so on.

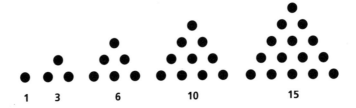

1   3   6   10   15

2 **Square numbers** are the result of squaring a number; that particular number of objects can be arranged in a square.

$$1^2 = 1 \qquad 2^2 = 4 \qquad 3^2 = 9 \qquad 4^2 = 16 \qquad 5^2 = \ldots \text{and so on}$$

so the square numbers are

1   4   9   16 . . . and so on

36 is a square number as can be seen here.

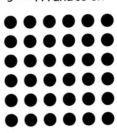

3 **Cube numbers** are simply those numbers resulting from cubing the counting numbers; and they are the number of unit cubes in a growing sequence of larger cubes.

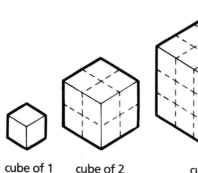 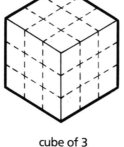 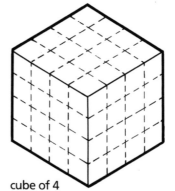

cube of 1   cube of 2   cube of 3   cube of 4

$1^3 = 1$ $2^3 = 8$ $3^3 = 27$ $4^3 = 64$ $5^3 = \ldots$ and so on

so the cube numbers are

1 8 27 64 . . . and so on

4 It is possible to have a sequence of numbers generated that depend upon a rule that uses previous numbers in the sequence. One famous sequence is called the **Fibonacci series**. In this series any number is the sum of the two before it. If we start with 1 and 1 we get

1 1 2 3 5 8 13 21 34 55 . . . and so on

5 If you have a series of numbers how do you try to discover the rule that is generating the numbers? One way is to look carefully to see if they are recognisable. Are they always odd, or even, or some other special sort of number (e.g. a multiple of 3)? Failing that, do the numbers differ from each other in a particular way? For example, what are the next two numbers in the following sequence?

1 2 4 7 11 16 22 ? ?

The answer is 29 and 37.

'We could start with any two numbers, but the principle is the same'

If we look at the differences between consecutive numbers, we can see that these differences increase steadily.

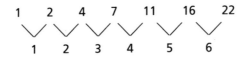

We can see from this that the next two numbers will be 29 and 37.

How to Do It

1
(i) Show that 28 is a triangular number.
(ii) If T_1 means the first triangular number, T_2 the second and T_3 the third triangular number, what is the result of $T_1 + T_2 + T_3$? Is the result a triangular number?

Solution

(i) There are two ways of solving this. One is by adding the counting numbers:

$$1+2+3+4+5+6+7 = 28 \quad \text{(so it is a triangular number)}$$

The other way is by a diagram:

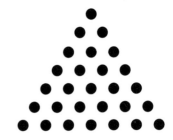

(ii) $T_1 + T_2 + T_3 = 1+3+6 = 10$

10 is the fourth triangular number.

2a Which of the following are square numbers?

(i) 144   (ii) 99   (iii) 49   (iv) 400

Solution

(i) $144 = 12^2$ so it is a square number.
(ii) 99 is not a square number ($9^2 = 81$ and $10^2 = 100$).
(iii) $49 = 7^2$ so it is a square number.
(iv) $400 = 20^2$ so it is a square number.

b The triangular number T_n is the nth triangular number. Find:

(i) $T_1 + T_2$ (ii) $T_6 + T_7$ (iii) $T_9 + T_{10}$

What type of numbers are the results?

Solution

(i) $T_1 + T_2 = 1 + 3 = 4$
(ii) $T_6 + T_7 = 21 + 28 = 49$
(iii) $T_9 + T_{10} = 45 + 55 = 100$

All of the answers are square numbers.
By drawing dotty diagrams of the numbers, you might show that this is so for the numbers given in the question. Note that the shape of the triangle of dots should be a right-angled one like this:

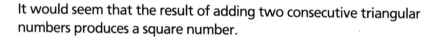

It would seem that the result of adding two consecutive triangular numbers produces a square number.

3 Which of the following numbers are cube numbers:

(i) 125   (ii) 343   (iii) 81   (iv) 1000

Solution

(i) $125 = 5^3$ so it is a cube number.
(ii) $343 = 7^3$ so it is a cube number.
(iii) 81 is not a cube number ($4^3 = 64$ and $5^3 = 125$).
(iv) $1000 = 10^3$ so it is a cube number.

4 a Consider the following four neighbouring Fibonacci numbers:

8   13   21   34

Multiply the outer pair and multiply the inner pair. What is the difference between the answers? Try it with another set of four neighbouring Fibonacci numbers – what do you notice?

Solution

The outer pair multiply to give 272, and the inner pair multiply to give 273. The difference is 1.

We try it again with another set of four Fibonacci numbers.

    55   89   144   233

The outer pair multiply to give 12 815, and the inner pair multiply to give 12 816. The difference is 1.

It begins to look as though the difference is always 1.

b What are the next five terms in a Fibonacci type sequence that starts with 1 and 3?

Solution

    1   3...4   7   11   18   29

c Here is a rule for generating the nth number in a series: $2n-1$. What is the product of the third and fifth terms?

Solution

$$\text{The third term} = 2(3) - 1 = 5$$
$$\text{The fifth term} = 2(5) - 1 = 9$$
$$\text{The product} = 9 \times 5 = 45$$

5 a Draw the next two patterns in the following two sequences:

(i)

(ii)

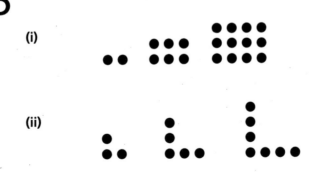

Solution

(ii)

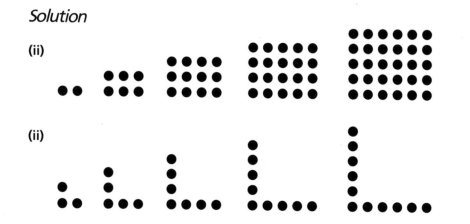

(ii)

b What is the formula for each of the patterns in question 5a?

Solution

(i) The numbers go

   2   6   12   20   30

There is no obvious pattern here – so look at the rectangles. The rectangles are

   1×2 2×3 3×4 4×5 5×6

so the formula is $n(n+1)$.

(ii) The numbers go

   3   5   7   9   11   (the odd numbers)

It is not so easy to state the formula from this, so look at the shape. The arms of the L shape each have n dots plus the corner one, so the formula is $2n+1$.

c Write down the first five terms of the sequences for each of the following rules:

(i) Start with 3, then keep adding 4.
(ii) Start with 1, then keep on doubling and add 1.
(iii) Start with 1, then keep on adding 1 and doubling.

'Note that the order is important; double and add 1 is not the same as add 1 and double'

Solution

(i) 3   7   11   15   19
(ii) 1   3   7   15   31
(iii) 1   4   10   22   46

CORNWALL COLLEGE
LEARNING CENTRE

Do It Yourself

1 Using the first six triangular numbers write down:

  (i) one that is a prime number;

  (ii) two that are multiples of 5;

  (iii) those that are not multiples of 3.

2 Extend the following number pattern to find 65^2 and 95^2:

$$5^2 = 0 \times 10 + 25 = 25$$
$$15^2 = 10 \times 20 + 25 = 225$$
$$25^2 = 20 \times 30 + 25 = 625$$

3 Find the cubes of the numbers 1 to 10. Which of these cubes are also square numbers? What is the next number after 10 whose cube is also a square number?

4 Janice makes the following pattern of squares using cocktail sticks:

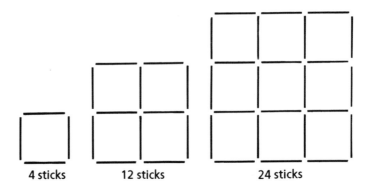

4 sticks   12 sticks   24 sticks

  (i) Draw the next square in the pattern. How many sticks are needed to make it?

  (ii) Continue the following number pattern with the next two terms:

$$1 \times 4 \quad 2 \times 6 \quad 3 \times 8$$

  Does this seem to be connected with the squares? If so, how?

  (iii) How many sticks would be needed for the sixth square in the series?

  (iv) Which square in the pattern uses 112 sticks?

5 **a** Write down the next two terms in each of the following sequences:

    (i) 3 6 9 12   (ii) 4 7 10 13

  (iii) 5 10 15   (iv) 20 17 14 11

b Here are the first seven terms in a sequence of numbers:

    3 5 8 12 17 23 30

  (i) Write down the next two terms of the sequence.

  (ii) Explain how you found the terms.

c Show that the sequence:

$$\frac{1}{2} \quad \frac{1+3}{2+4} \quad \frac{1+3+5}{2+4+6} \quad \frac{1+3+5+7}{2+4+6+8} \quad \frac{1+3+5+7+9}{2+4+6+8+10} \text{ and so on}$$

is actually the same as

$$\frac{1}{2} \quad \frac{2}{3} \quad \frac{3}{4} \quad \frac{4}{5} \quad \frac{5}{6} \text{ and so on.}$$

Using this, what do you think is the value of:

$$\frac{1+3+5+7+9+\ldots+197+199}{2+4+6+8+\ldots+198+200}$$

Try to give a reason for your answer.

> *'Numbers may seem to be just an endless string of figures, but if you know where to look there are all sorts of hidden patterns to be found'*

3 | Fractions

Things You Need to Know

1 **Fractions** are a way of saying that something is a part of some whole amount. For example, the fraction $\frac{1}{4}$ means one part out of four equal parts into which the whole is divided. The '1' is called the numerator and the '4' the denominator.

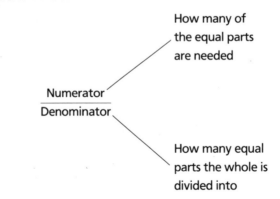

How many of the equal parts are needed

$$\frac{\text{Numerator}}{\text{Denominator}}$$

How many equal parts the whole is divided into

2 **Equivalent fractions** are those fractions which represent the same amount even though the numbers are different. For example, $\frac{1}{4}$ and $\frac{2}{8}$ are equivalent fractions. It is easy to produce equivalent fractions – just *multiply the numerator and the denominator by the same number.*

3 Whenever possible, we simplify fractions – that is, write them in the simplest form, or the **lowest possible terms**. To do this we reverse the idea of equivalent fractions and see if the numerator and the denominator have any common factors – if so, we divide by the common factor and repeat the process.

$$\frac{28}{42} = \frac{14}{21} \quad \text{(dividing numerator and denominator by 2)}$$

$$= \frac{2}{3} \quad \text{(and then dividing by 7)}$$

'Before you can add or subtract fractions, they all have to have the same denominator'

4 When the numerator is larger than the denominator, we call it an **improper fraction**. For example, $\frac{5}{4}$ is an improper fraction.

5 A **mixed number** is a combination of a fraction and a whole number and represents the same thing as an improper fraction. For example:

$$\frac{5}{4} = 1\frac{1}{4}$$

To go from a mixed number to an improper fraction, remember that the denominator tells you how many pieces are required to make whole ones, so simply multiply the whole number by the denominator to find how much the whole is worth and then add on the numerator of the fraction. For example:

$$3\frac{5}{7} = \frac{21}{7} + \frac{5}{7} = \frac{26}{7}$$

Going from an improper fraction to a mixed number is just the reverse – divide the numerator by the denominator to give the whole part, then the remainder gives the numerator for the mixed number. For example:

$$\frac{25}{6} = 4 + \frac{1}{6} = 4\frac{1}{6}$$

Improper fractions are usually converted into mixed numbers.

6 **Adding** and **subtracting fractions** is easy to do if you remember to convert the fractions to the same sort – in other words with the same denominator. Choose a new denominator which is the smallest number divisible by the denominators of both fractions. (This is known as the **lowest common multiple**, or **LCM**. For example, to add $\frac{2}{3}$ and $\frac{1}{4}$, we need to change each fraction into twelfths.

$$\frac{2}{3} + \frac{1}{4} = \frac{8}{12} + \frac{3}{12} \quad \text{(12 is the smallest number divisible by 3 and 4)}$$

$$= \frac{11}{12} \quad \text{(sometimes we can cancel this down – but not here)}$$

The method is identical for subtraction – except that you subtract!

"It is often useful to know some of the simpler fractions and their decimal equivalents, like 0.25 and $\frac{1}{4}$, 0.5 and $\frac{1}{2}$, and 0.75 and $\frac{3}{4}$"

7 Fractions and decimals can be thought of as different ways of representing the same thing. For example, half of something is $\frac{1}{2}$ as a fraction and 0.5 as a decimal. Converting from fractions to decimals is just a matter of seeing the fraction as a division sum and writing the answer in decimal form, remembering that any whole number goes before the decimal point. For example:

$$3\frac{13}{20} = 3.65 \quad \text{(use a calculator to divide 13 by 20)}$$

(For how to convert decimals to fractions, see page 37.)

8 When some fractions are converted to decimals the division continues in a never-ending manner and the sequence just repeats itself. The most common **recurring decimal** is $\frac{1}{3}$, which becomes 0.333 333 333 333 333 333 3 . . . and so on. This would be written down as 0.$\dot{3}$. Some have a repeating pattern of digits; for example:

$$\frac{1}{7} = 0.142857142857142857\ldots$$

$$= 0.\dot{1}4285\dot{7}$$

How to Do It

1 If John baked 12 cakes and Sally ate 4 of them, what fraction of the original cakes is left?

Solution

There are now 8 cakes left out of the original 12, so the fraction is

$$\frac{8}{12} = \frac{2}{3}$$

2 Using a diagram show that $\frac{3}{4}$ is the same as $\frac{6}{8}$.

Solution

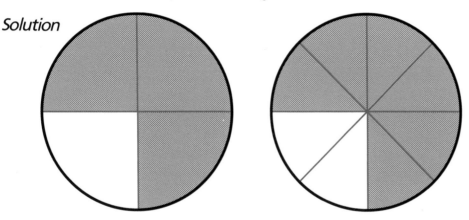

3 Convert the following fractions to their lowest terms. If a fraction cannot be reduced, write 'already in its lowest terms'.

(i) $\frac{27}{45}$ (ii) $\frac{7}{24}$ (iii) $\frac{36}{96}$

Solution

(i) $\frac{27}{45} = \frac{3}{5}$ (dividing top/bottom by 9)

(ii) $\frac{7}{24}$ already in its lowest terms

(There is no common divisor of 7 and 24.)

(iii) $\frac{36}{96} = \frac{12}{32}$ (dividing top/bottom by 3)

$ = \frac{3}{8}$ (further dividing by 4)

31

4 Write the following mixed numbers as improper fractions:

(i) $2\frac{1}{2}$ (ii) $4\frac{3}{8}$ (iii) $3\frac{4}{7}$

Solution

(i) $2\frac{1}{2} = \frac{4}{2} + \frac{1}{2}$

$= \frac{5}{2}$

(ii) $4\frac{3}{8} = \frac{32}{8} + \frac{3}{8}$

$= \frac{35}{8}$

(iii) $3\frac{4}{7} = \frac{21}{7} + \frac{4}{7}$

$= \frac{25}{7}$

5 Convert each of the following improper fractions into mixed numbers:

(i) $\frac{19}{4}$ (ii) $\frac{26}{9}$ (iii) $\frac{33}{7}$ (iv) $\frac{45}{3}$

Solution

(i) $\frac{19}{4} = 4\frac{3}{4}$

(ii) $\frac{26}{9} = 2\frac{8}{9}$

(iii) $\frac{33}{7} = 4\frac{5}{7}$

(iv) $\frac{45}{3} = 15$

'Using a calculator helps to find the whole number part of the mixed number'

6 **a** Find the value of $3\frac{1}{2} - 2\frac{1}{3} + 4\frac{1}{5}$.

Solution

The lowest common multiple of 3, 2 and 5 is 30, so convert to thirtieths:

$$3\frac{1}{2} - 2\frac{1}{3} + 4\frac{1}{5} = \frac{7}{2} - \frac{7}{3} + \frac{21}{5} = \frac{7 \times 15}{2 \times 15} - \frac{7 \times 10}{3 \times 10} + \frac{21 \times 6}{5 \times 6}$$

$$= \frac{105 - 70 + 126}{30} = \frac{161}{30}$$

$$= 5\frac{11}{30}$$

b Alan, Brenda and Chris started a joint business. In the first year their profits were £18 000. Alan received $\frac{2}{5}$ of the profit, Brenda received $\frac{1}{3}$ of the profit and Chris received the rest of the profit. How much did each receive?

Solution

Alan: $\frac{2}{5}$ of £18 000 $= £\dfrac{36\,000}{5}$

$= £7200$

Brenda: $\frac{1}{3}$ of £18 000 $= £\dfrac{18\,000}{3}$

$= £6000$

Chris: £18 000 $-$ (£7200 + £6000) $=$ £4800

7 For the following sum:

   (i) Work through it in fractions and convert the fraction answer to a decimal.

   (ii) Change each of the fractions to decimals and work out the answer as a decimal.

   (iii) Do both methods of finding an answer give the same answer?

$$1\frac{3}{8} + 2\frac{3}{5}$$

Solution

(i) $1\frac{3}{8} + 2\frac{3}{5} = \frac{11}{8} + \frac{13}{5} = \frac{11 \times 5}{8 \times 5} + \frac{13 \times 8}{5 \times 8}$

$= \frac{55 + 104}{40} = \frac{159}{40} = 3\frac{39}{40}$

$= 3.975$

(ii) $1\frac{3}{8} + 2\frac{3}{5} = 1.375 + 2.6$

$= 3.975$

(iii) Yes, the two answers are the same.

8 **a** Both of the fractions $\frac{1}{11}$ and $\frac{1}{9}$ produce recurring decimals. Add the fractions together and convert the fractional answer to a decimal. What do you notice about the answer?

Solution

$\frac{1}{11} + \frac{1}{9} = \frac{1 \times 9 + 1 \times 11}{99} = \frac{20}{99}$

$= 0.202\,020\,20 \dots$

It is a recurring decimal too.

b What is this recurring decimal as a fraction?

$0.245\,245\,245 \dots$

Solution
Let's call the recurring fraction r

$r = 0.245\,245\,245 \dots$

As the fraction repeats in groups of 3, multiply by 1000, so

$1000r = 245.245\,245 \dots$

but

$r = 0.245\,245 \dots$

so, subtracting these gives:

$999r = 245$

$r = \frac{245}{999}$

c Express the recurring decimal 0.272 727 272 7 . . . as a fraction in its simplest form.

Solution

Let y be the recurring decimal 0.272 727 2727 . . .

$$y = 0.272\,727\,2727\ldots$$
$$100y = 27.272\,727\,2727\ldots$$

Subtract y:

$$99y = 27$$
$$y = \frac{27}{99}$$
$$y = \frac{3}{11}$$

Do It Yourself

1 For each of the shapes below, write down the fraction shaded and the fraction unshaded – both in their simplest form.

(i)   (ii)   (iii)   (iv)

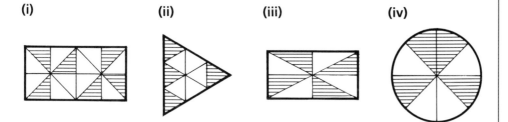

2 A toolkit has spanners in the following sizes:

$$\frac{5}{8} \quad \frac{1}{2} \quad \frac{1}{8} \quad \frac{9}{16} \quad \frac{3}{8} \quad \frac{1}{4} \quad \frac{5}{16} \quad \frac{7}{8} \quad \frac{7}{16} \quad \frac{3}{4} \quad \frac{11}{16}$$

Write each fraction in sixteenths and rearrange them in order of size, smallest to largest. Write your answer in the original form, not sixteenths.

3 Where possible, write each of the following fractions in its simplest form:

$$\frac{6}{8} \quad \frac{9}{27} \quad \frac{6}{20} \quad \frac{4}{18} \quad \frac{14}{35} \quad \frac{75}{150}$$

4 18 tea cakes are to be divided equally among 5 people. How much does each person get? Write your answer as an improper fraction and as a mixed number.

5 A group of people have shared some loaves. If each person received $2\frac{3}{7}$ loaves, by changing this to an improper fraction what is the smallest number of people in the group, and what is the smallest number of whole loaves that were shared?

6 **a** Work out the following:

(i) $\dfrac{2}{3}+\dfrac{1}{5}$ (ii) $\dfrac{3}{4}+\dfrac{1}{10}$ (iii) $\dfrac{3}{5}-\dfrac{1}{7}$ (iv) $\dfrac{4}{9}-\dfrac{1}{6}$

b Swareen wants to buy a hi-fi costing £135.99. Her father says he will give her $\frac{1}{3}$ of the cost providing she saves the rest. How much does Swareen need to save?

7 Express each of the following as a decimal:

(i) $\dfrac{17}{25}$ (ii) $7\dfrac{5}{12}$ (iii) $12\dfrac{19}{40}$

8 Find the simplest fraction for:

(i) 0.545 454 54 . . .

(ii) 0.111 111 . . .

Decimals, Percentages and Ratios

4

Things You Need to Know

1 **Decimals** are just a way of writing fractions that have 10, or 100, or 1000, or 10 000, and so on, as the denominator. So we have:

$$\frac{7}{10} \text{ is } 0.7 \qquad \frac{63}{100} \text{ is } 0.63 \qquad \frac{149}{100} \text{ is } 1.49 \quad \text{and so on}$$

For a fraction that does not have 10, 100, 1000, etc as its denominator, just divide the denominator into the numerator.

$$\frac{5}{8} = 0.625$$

Converting a decimal to a fraction is just a matter of putting the 10, or 100, or 1000 value as the denominator of the fraction and then cancelling if possible:

$$0.52 = \frac{52}{100} \quad \text{(cancel by dividing by 4)}$$
$$= \frac{13}{25}$$

(For how to convert fractions to decimals, see page 30.)

'The percentage sign is nothing more than a shorthand version of writing 'out of 100'

2 **Percentage** means 'out of 100', so if you achieved a mark of 80 out of a possible 100 for an examination your result would be 80%; it can also be thought of as a fraction with 100 as the denominator and the percentage figure as the numerator.

A different way of writing a percentage is as a decimal:

$$23\% = \frac{23}{100} = 0.23$$

3 Percentages are useful for comparing and to do this we often have to turn a fraction into a percentage. To do this we just multiply the fraction by 100%.

$$\frac{16}{20} = \frac{16}{20} \times 100\% = 80\%$$

4 If you have to find what percentage something is of something else they have to be in the same units. For example, what percentage is 150 mm of 1 metre?

$$1 \text{ metre} = 1000 \text{ mm}$$

so

$$150 \text{ mm} = \frac{150}{1000} \times 100\% = \frac{150}{10} \times 1\%$$
$$= 15\%$$

5 **Ratio** is a comparison of sizes. For example, if you build a model in which the scale is 1 : 50, this means that everything in the real world is 50 times larger than on the model.

Sometimes we wish to divide up something in a particular ratio. For example, if three children divide a bag of 48 sweets up in the ratio of 3 : 4 : 5, to find how many sweets each child gets, we must find the total number of parts that the bag of sweets is being divided into. This is

$$3 + 4 + 5 = 12$$

As there are 48 sweets that means that each part is 4 sweets. So

> The first child gets 3 parts or 12 sweets
> The second child gets 4 parts or 16 sweets
> The third child gets 5 parts or 20 sweets

We could have written the ratio as $12:16:20$. However, it is a lot easier if this is cancelled down (by dividing the terms by 4) to give $3:4:5$.

How to Do It

1 a Convert each of the following fractions into decimals:

(i) $\dfrac{7}{10}$ (ii) $\dfrac{43}{100}$ (iii) $\dfrac{3}{8}$ (iv) $\dfrac{7}{15}$

Solution
Using a calculator (where necessary):

(i) 0.7 (ii) 0.43 (iii) 0.375 (iv) 0.4667 (4 d.p.)

b Convert each of the following decimals to fractions in their simplest form:

(i) 0.625 (ii) 0.05 (iii) 0.37

Solution

(i) $0.625 = \dfrac{625}{1000}$ (now cancel by dividing by 25)

$\qquad = \dfrac{25}{40}$ (now cancel by dividing by 5)

$\qquad = \dfrac{5}{8}$

(ii) $0.05 = \dfrac{5}{100}$ (now cancel by dividing by 5)

$\qquad = \dfrac{1}{20}$

(iii) $0.37 = \dfrac{37}{100}$ (nothing to cancel now)

'Decimals are special sorts of fractions based around dividing by 10'

2 a Harry took three examinations in mathematics. In the first he scored 28 out of 40, in the second he scored 23 out of 35 and in the third he scored 19 out of 25. The overall mark is obtained by adding the marks together and giving this as a percentage of the total maximum marks.

> (i) What is the maximum marks he could have got?
> (ii) What mark did he actually get?
> (iii) What is this mark as a percentage of the maximum?

Solution

(i) The maximum is $40 + 35 + 25 = 100$ marks.

(ii) Harry got $28 + 23 + 19 = 70$ marks.

(iii) This is 70%.

b Convert the following percentages into decimals:

> (i) 75%   (ii) 5%   (iii) $67\frac{1}{2}$%

Solution

(i) $75\% = \dfrac{75}{100} = 0.75$

(ii) $5\% = \dfrac{5}{100} = 0.05$

(iii) $67\frac{1}{2}\% = \dfrac{67\frac{1}{2}}{100} = \dfrac{67.5}{100} = 0.675$

3 a In question 2a Harry took three mathematics examinations and scored:

> (i) 28 out of 40 in the first examination;
> (ii) 23 out of 35 in the second;
> (iii) 19 out of 25 in the third.

Convert each of the results into a percentage figure and find Harry's average percentage mark for these examinations.

Solution

(i) $\dfrac{28}{40} = 70\%$

(ii) $\dfrac{23}{35} = 66\%$ (to the nearest whole value)

(iii) $\dfrac{19}{25} = 76\%$

The average of these is $(70 + 66 + 76) \div 3 = 71\%$ (to the nearest whole value).

b If you got 15 out of 20 for one test and 18 out of 25 for another, which is the better mark?

Solution

$$\dfrac{15}{20} = \dfrac{15}{20} \times 100\%$$

$$= \dfrac{15}{1} \times 5\% \text{ (cancelling by 20)}$$

$$= 75\%$$

$$\dfrac{18}{25} = \dfrac{18}{25} \times 100\%$$

$$= \dfrac{18}{1} \times 4\% \text{ (cancelling by 25)}$$

$$= 72\%$$

So we can see that 15 out of 20 is better than 18 out of 25.

4a A dealer in antiques always makes a profit of 30% on her sales. She buys a desk for £180; what must be her selling price?

Solution

There are two possible ways to solve this: find the profit and add on to the selling price or use the fact that the selling price is 130% of the buying price.

Method 1

Profit $= 30\%$ of £180 $=$ £54
so selling price $=$ £180 $+$ £54 $=$ £234

Method 2

Selling price $= 130\%$ of £180 $=$ £234

"Make sure you can use the % button on your calculator – it can save a lot of time and trouble"

b The value of Anna's mum's car decreases by 20% each year. If her car was originally worth £10 000, how much will it be worth after 5 years?

Solution

Value at start of year 1 = £10 000   Loss = 20% of £10 000 = £2000
Value at start of year 2 = £8000   Loss = 20% of £8000   = £1600
Value at start of year 3 = £6400   Loss = 20% of £6400   = £1280
Value at start of year 4 = £5120   Loss = 20% of £5120   = £1024
Value at start of year 5 = £4096   Loss = 20% of £4096   = £819.20
Value at end of year 5   = £3276.80

c Jane's dad's vegetable garden is a rectangular plot 25 m long and 15 m wide. He increases the length by 15% and decreases the width by 5%. What is the change in area in square metres? Express this as a percentage of the original area.

Solution
Method 1

New length = 100% + 15% of the old length
$\qquad$ = 115% × 25 m
$\qquad$ = 28.75 m
New width = 100% − 5% of the old width
$\qquad$ = 95% × 15 m
$\qquad$ = 14.25 m
Old area = 25 m × 15 m
$\qquad$ = 375 m²
New area = 28.75 m × 14.25 m
$\qquad$ = 409.7 m²   (1 d.p.)
Change in area = 34.7 m²

As a percentage of the original area, change in area is

$$\frac{34.7}{375} \times 100\% = 9.3\% \quad (1\ \text{d.p.})$$

Method 2

As new length $= 115\%$ of old length (that is, 1.15 times bigger)
and new width $= 95\%$ of old width (that is, 0.95 of old width)
then new area $= 1.15 \times 0.95$ of old area
$\qquad\qquad = 1.0925$ of old area (by calculator)
$\qquad\qquad = 109.25\%$ of old area

So new area is 9.25% bigger than old area or 9.3% (1 d.p.)

5 a A health club has men and women members in the ratio $4:5$. The club has 196 men; how many members does it have?

Solution

Men : women $= 4:5$ (a total of 9 parts)

So 4 parts represent 196 members, hence 1 part is 49 members. So the complete membership (the 9 parts) is

$9 \times 49 = 441$ members

b A piece of wood is to be divided up into three parts in the ratio of $2:3:5$. If its length is 1.5 m how long will the shortest piece be?

Solution
The total of the parts is

$2+3+5 = 10$

So 10 parts are equal to 1.5 m (or 150 cm), hence 1 part is 15 cm. The smallest piece is 2 parts long and so is

$2 \times 15\,\text{cm} = 30\,\text{cm}$

c Asir and Benny inherit some money from an uncle. The amounts are in the ratio of $3:5$; if Asir receives £1500 how much does Benny get?

Solution
The £1500 must represent the 3 parts that Asir receives, so 1 part is

£1500 $\div 3 =$ £500

Since Benny receives 5 parts then Benny gets

$5 \times$ £500 $=$ £2500

Do It Yourself

1 **a** Convert the following fractions into decimals:

(i) $\dfrac{9}{10}$ (ii) $\dfrac{57}{100}$ (iii) $\dfrac{205}{1000}$ (iv) $\dfrac{7}{100}$ (careful!)

(v) $\dfrac{3}{4}$ (vi) $\dfrac{3}{5}$ (vii) $\dfrac{13}{20}$ (viii) $\dfrac{39}{40}$

b Convert the following decimals into fractions in their simplest form:

(i) 0.56 (ii) 0.88 (iii) 0.12 (iv) 0.05

2 Convert the following percentages into decimals:

(i) 27% (ii) 65% (iii) 40% (iv) 8%

3 Rearrange the following list of fractions in order, smallest first, by changing each fraction into a percentage:

$\dfrac{5}{8}$ $\dfrac{7}{11}$ $\dfrac{13}{20}$ $\dfrac{3}{5}$ $\dfrac{1}{2}$

4 **a** In a sale, prices are reduced by 15%. How much does Anne pay for a coat marked at £55.00?

b Ace Bargain Company allow a $3\frac{1}{2}$% discount for a cash sale. What is the cash price of an article marked at £23.00?

c Currently VAT (see page 46) is 17.5%. Find the full price (to the nearest penny) of the following items:

(i) A sofa-bed   £199 + VAT
(ii) A CD player   £90 + VAT
(iii) A badminton racquet   £31.50 + VAT

d The dimensions of a rectangle are measured to the nearest millimetre, but they are quoted to the nearest centimetre. Its length is quoted at 8 cm and its width as 5 cm.

  (i) What is the greatest length it could be?
  (ii) What is the greatest width it could be?
  (iii) What is the greatest area it could be?
  (iv) How much bigger is this area than the area of the quoted size?
  (v) What is the difference in area as a percentage of the quoted size area?

e A dealer bought a car for £5000 and sold it at a profit of 20%. The buyer later sold it back to the dealer for 20% less than he paid for it. How much did the buyer get when he resold the car?

5

a (i) Divide £45 in the ratio 2 : 3.
  (ii) Divide 42 m in the ratio 4 : 3.
  (iii) Divide 63 kg in the ratio 2 : 3 : 4.

b 'No Mess,' the new wonder washing powder, has three main ingredients, known as Spotto, Marko and Soapo, in the ratio 4 : 2 : 1 by weight. A box of 'No Mess' contains 0.8 kg of Marko; what is the weight of the box of 'No Mess'?

c The screen of a television is measured by the length of the diagonal. The ratio of the width of the screen to the diagonal is 4 : 5.

  (i) What is the width of a 14-inch screen?
  (ii) What size screen has a width of 15.2 inches?

5 | Practical Maths

Things You Need to Know

1 Anyone who earns money has to pay the government part of their earnings to help pay for the running of the country – this is called **income tax**. Everyone has an amount that they are allowed to earn before they have to start paying tax – this is known as the **personal allowance**. Everything above this amount is taxed. Tax is usually expressed as a percentage, typically 25%.

Another form of tax is **VAT**, or value added tax, which is put on the price of some goods. It is calculated as a percentage of the price (currently $17\frac{1}{2}$ per cent).

2 **Interest** is the term used to describe either the extra money paid when you borrow money, or the extra money earned by your money in the building society. It is usually expressed as a percentage of the original amount (e.g. 6%). Interest is usually paid yearly, or 'per annum'.

3 There are two different types of interest. In the case of **simple interest** the interest is worked out each year on the money and this is then kept separate.

4 In the case of **compound interest** the interest gets added to the current amount and so the amount of interest increases each year.

5 **Hire purchase** (HP) is a way of buying goods by borrowing the money and paying it back gradually with regular payments, and often an initial deposit is required. Naturally, this will cost more than the original goods since interest has to be paid on the money borrowed.

How to Do It

1 a Sally earns £19 450 per annum. If her personal allowance is £3800 and the tax rate is 25%, how much does she pay in tax each year?

Solution
Sally is taxed on

$$£19 450 - £3800 = £15 650$$

She pays

$$25\% \times £15 650 \text{ in tax} = £3912.50$$

b Mustapha has a tax allowance of £4200. His salary is £23 300 per annum. Tax is levied at 25%. If he pays his tax in 12 equal monthly payments, how much tax does he pay per month?

Solution
Mustapha is taxed on

$$£23 300 - £4200 = £19 100$$

Tax paid over the year is

$$25\% \times £19 100 = £4775$$

So each month he pays

$$£4775 \div 12 = £397.92 \quad \text{(to the nearest penny)}$$

2a If Sharon invests £600 for one year at 8% per annum, what does she get back?

Solution
It earns

$$£600 \times 8\% \text{ interest} = £48$$

So the amount she gets back at the end of the year is £648.

b Ian invests £500 for one year and receives £550 at the end of the year. What is the annual rate of interest?

Solution
Interest earned is

$$£550 - £500 = £50$$

Interest rate is

$$\frac{50}{500} \times 100 = 10\% \text{ per annum}$$

'The rate of interest is the percentage of the initial loan you are charged for every year'

3a If Sam borrows £250 for 3 years at 8% per annum simple interest, how much does he have to pay back?

Solution
Each year the interest is

$$£250 \times 8\% = £20$$

But he borrows it for 3 years so the total interest is

$$3 \times £20 = £60$$

So he has to pay back

$$£250 + £60 = £310.$$

b £200 is invested at 7% p.a. simple interest. How much does it amount to after 3 years?

Solution

Interest each year is

$$7\% \times £200 = £14.00$$

So simple interest for 3 years is

$$3 \times £14.00 = £42.00$$

Hence amount $= £242$.

c Denise invests £1000 at $6\frac{1}{2}\%$ p.a. simple interest. When she withdraws all her money it has grown to £1260; for how many years did she leave it invested?

Solution

Interest earned each year is

$$6\tfrac{1}{2}\% \times £1000 = £65$$

Interest earned is

$$£1260 - £1000 = £260$$

So number of years $= 4$ years.

4 a If Sam borrows £250 for 3 years at 8% per annum compound interest, how much does he have to pay back?

Solution

At the start of year 1 Sam borrows £250
Interest for year 1 $= £250 \times 8\% = £20$
At the end of year 1 he owes £250 + £20 $= £270$

At the start of year 2 he owes £270
Interest for year 2 $= £270 \times 8\% = £21.60$
At the end of year 2 he owes £270 + £21.60 $= £291.60$

At the start of year 3 he owes £291.60
Interest for year 3 $= £291.60 \times 8\% = £23.33$ (to the nearest penny)
At the end of year 3 he owes £314.93

So he has to pay back £314.93 (nearly £5.00 more than if it were simple interest).

b £400 is left in the Maths County Building Society where it earns 8% compound interest p.a. How many complete years must it be left for it to become over £500?

Solution

Start of year 1 the amount = £400
Interest earned in year 1 = 8% × £400 = £32

Start of year 2 the amount = £432
Interest earned in year 2 = 8% × £432 = £34.56

Start of year 3 the amount = £466.56
Interest earned in year 3 = 8% × £466.56 = £37.32

Start of year 4 the amount = £503.88

So it takes 3 years for it to amount to over £500.

'Always remember you have to compare the cash price with the hire purchase price'

5 A video recorder is priced at £349.99. The shop selling it offers a hire purchase scheme requiring a deposit of £70 and 12 monthly payments of £26.50. How much extra is paid if it is purchased using hire purchase?

Solution

Firstly the deposit has to be paid = £70
Now 12 payments of £26.50 = £318

The total paid is

£318 + £70 = £388

The extra to be paid is

£388 − £349.99 = £38.01

Do It Yourself

1 In a year Jo paid £4800 in tax. Tax was charged at 25% and her tax allowance was £4500. What was her salary that year?

2 Wayne borrowed £345 to buy a video recorder. He paid the amount back over a year and realised he had actually paid £390 altogether. What was the interest rate per annum?

3ª Find the simple interest paid on £480 for 4 years at 5% per annum.

b John receives a present of £80 and decides to put it into the bank, where it earns simple interest at a rate of 11% per annum. How many years must he leave it in the bank to receive £44 interest?

4 Harry has £400 to invest for a period of 3 years. He could invest it at $12\frac{1}{2}$% p.a. simple interest or 10% p.a. compound interest. Which is the better investment and by how much is it better?

5 In order to borrow £18 000 from the Bricklayers Building Society the repayments are £12.50 per calendar month per £1000 borrowed for 10 years.

  (i) Calculate the monthly payment.
  (ii) How much interest is paid over the 10 years?

6 Scale, Maps and Bearings

Things You Need to Know

1 The **scale** tells us how much bigger (or smaller) the real thing is compared to the scaled object. It is written as the length of the model compared to the length of the real thing and is used mainly for models, maps, scale drawings and such like. For example:

$$1:30 \quad or \quad 1 \text{ to } 30 \quad or \quad \frac{1}{30} \quad or \quad 1\text{ cm represents } 30\text{ cm}$$

Since a map often covers a large area the scale is often quite small, e.g. some Ordnance Survey maps have a scale of 1 : 50 000 – on a map like this a house is generally a small dot.

2 It is often much more convenient to produce a **scale drawing** of the situation and work with the drawing than to work with the real situation. Imagine trying to plan a new kitchen by pulling around the cooker, the sink and all the other fittings – it is so much easier with a scale drawing.

HOW TO DO IT

3 With maps, besides the scale there is an additional aspect – the direction or **bearing** of one point from another. The bearing is always given as a three-figure number that describes the angle that has to be turned through if you face north and turn *clockwise* to face the required direction. For example:

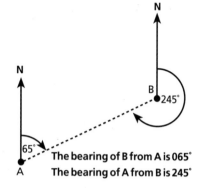

The bearing of B from A is 065°
The bearing of A from B is 245°

'*Note that the bearing of B from A and the bearing of A from B differ by 180°, so if you know one of them it is just a matter of adding or subtracting 180°*'

4 Using the scale on a map is just a matter of measuring the distance on the map between the two places and, using the scale, converting this figure to the full-size measurement. For example, on the map of the Isle of Wight the distance from Ventnor to Cowes is measured as 4.2 cm. This means that the real life distance is

$4.2 \times 4\,km = 16.8\,km$

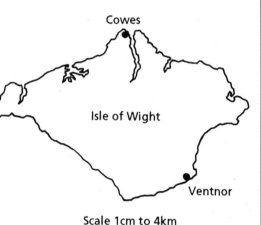

Cowes

Isle of Wight

Ventnor

Scale 1cm to 4km

How to Do It

1 The distance between two towns on a map is 5.2 km, and on the map it is 20.8 cm. What is the scale of the map? Give your answer both in terms of centimetres and kilometres and also as a ratio.

Solution

20.8 cm represents 5.2 km so 1 cm represents $\dfrac{5.2}{20.8} = 0.25\,km$.

So 1 cm represents

$0.25 \times 1000 \times 100\,cm = 25\,000\,cm$

So the scale is 1 : 25 000.

53

> *'Scale is simply the ratio of the length on a model to the length on the real thing'*

2 A plan of a rectangular room has a scale of 1 : 8. The room is 12 ft by 16 ft. What is its size on the plan?

Solution

A scale of 1 : 8 means that 1 ft represents 8 ft or $\frac{1}{8}$ ft represents 1 ft.

So 12 ft is represented by

$$12 \times \frac{1}{8}\,\text{ft} = 1.5\,\text{ft}$$

and 16 ft is represented by

$$16 \times \frac{1}{8}\,\text{ft} = 2\,\text{ft}$$

So the room dimensions on the plan are 1.5 ft × 2 ft (or 18 in × 24 in).

> *'A bearing is a way of giving a direction'*

3 Explorers in the Sahara desert leave their base camp. They travel north for 30 km, then 048° for 15 km and finally 30 km on a bearing of 102°. How far are they from base camp, and what is its bearing? (Use a scale of 1 cm to 10 km.)

Solution
From the drawing you get:

Distance from base camp = 50 km
on a bearing of 233°.

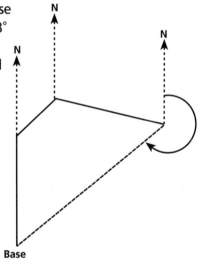

Base

4 The map shows part of Hertfordshire with some of the roads shown. From Harpenden, what is the straightline distance to the main towns? For each of them indicate the approximate direction using the eight points of the compass (N, NE, E, SE, S, SW, W, NW).

Solution

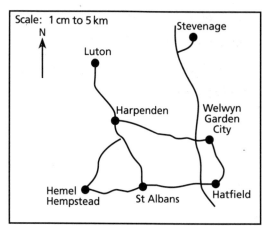

Scale: 1 cm to 5 km

From Harpenden to:

Luton – map distance = 1.6 cm
true distance = 1.6 × 5 km
= 8.0 km
Direction approximately North

Stevenage – map distance = 3.1 cm
true distance = 3.1 × 5 km
= 15.5 km
Direction approximately North East

W.G.C. – map distance = 2.7 cm
true distance = 2.7 × 5 km
= 13.5 km
Direction approximately East

Hatfield – map distance = 3.3 cm
true distance = 3.3 × 5 km
= 16.5 km
Direction approximately South East

St. Albans – map distance = 1.9 cm
true distance = 1.9 × 5 km
= 9.5 km
Direction approximately South

Hemel Hempstead – map distance = 2.0 cm
true distance = 2.0 × 5 km
= 10.0 km
Direction approximately South West

Do It Yourself

1 A model of a room has a scale of 2 cm to 0.25 m. The height of the model is 24 cm, its floor area is 700 cm² and its volume is 16 800 cm³. Find the height, the floor area and the volume of the room.

2 A coastguard on a cliff top 50 m high sees a boat out at sea at an angle of depression of 10°. By doing a scale drawing find how far the boat is from the foot of the cliffs. (Assume that the cliff face is vertical.)

'An angle of depression is the angle below a horizontal line'

'It's easier to do your scale drawing on graph paper'

3 A group of hikers walk 100 m on a bearing of 080° and then 200 m on a bearing of 150°. Draw an accurate scale drawing of the route. By taking measurements from your scale drawing find out how far they have to go to return directly to their start point and the bearing they must travel along.

4 On the map of the Isle of Wight (shown below) the most southerly point is called St Catherine's Point. How far is it from St Catherine's Point to:

    (i) Ventnor   (ii) Cowes

What is the bearing of these places from St. Catherine's Point?

Scale
1 cm to 4 km

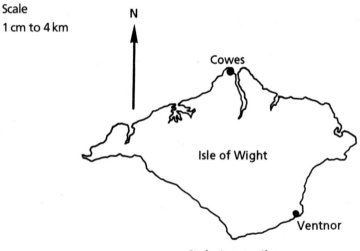

Scale 1cm to 4km

Mass, Length and Capacity

Things You Need to Know

1 The metric system uses the gram (g) as the basic unit of **mass**, or **weight**. Its connections with other weights in the metric system are:

$$1\,g = 1000 \text{ milligrams (or mg)}$$
$$1000\,g = 1 \text{ kilogram (or kg)}$$
$$1000\,kg = 1 \text{ tonne (or t)}$$

You ought to remember that 1 kg is about 2.2 lb in the imperial system and 1 lb is about 450 g.

2 The main unit for **length** is the metre (m). It is connected with other lengths as follows:

$$1\,m = 1000 \text{ millimetres (or mm)}$$
$$1000\,m = 1 \text{ kilometre (or km)}$$

There is also the centimetre:

$$1\,m = 100\,cm$$
$$1\,cm = 10\,mm$$

1 in is a little over 2.5 cm (or 25 mm); 1 ft is about 30 cm (or 300 mm); 1 m is just a little under 40 in.

3 Litres (l) are the unit of **capacity** in the metric system:

1 litre = 100 centilitres (cl)
1 litre = 1000 millilitres (ml)
1 cl = 10 ml

1 litre is a little over $1\frac{3}{4}$ pints (just remember it is less than 2 pints).

How to Do It

'The metric tonne is not the same as the imperial ton'

1 The mass of 1 cm³ of lead is 11.4 g. What is the mass of a piece of lead shaped as a rectangular box with measurements of
50 mm × 120 mm × 150 mm?

Solution
Since the mass of lead has been given for a cubic centimetre it makes sense to convert the original measurements into centimetres. They become:

5 cm × 12 cm × 15 cm

The volume is

5 × 12 × 15 = 900 cm³

The mass is

11.4 × 900 = 10 260 g = 10.26 kg

2a A ream of paper (500 sheets) is 6 cm thick. Find the thickness of one sheet of paper in millimetres.

Solution
As there are 500 sheets and their overall thickness is 6 cm (60 mm) then the thickness of one sheet is:

$$\frac{60}{500} = 0.12\,mm$$

b A 10 kg ingot of an alloy has a volume of 2000 cm³ and is going to be made into identical cylinders each of mass 50 g and cross-sectional area of 2 cm². How long will each cylinder be?

Solution

First find out how many cylinders there will be. Number of cylinders is

$$\frac{10\,\text{kg}}{50\,\text{g}} = \frac{10 \times 1000\,\text{g}}{50\,\text{g}} = 200$$

So volume of each cylinder is

$$\frac{1}{200}\,\text{of ingot volume} = \frac{1}{200} \times 2000\,\text{cm}^3 = 10\,\text{cm}^3$$

Volume of cylinder = area of cross-section × height

i.e. $10\,\text{cm}^3 = 2\,\text{cm}^2 \times \text{height}$

Height = 5 cm

3 How many 25 ml servings can you get from a bottle of lemonade which contains 1.7 litres?

Solution

Number of servings is

$$\frac{1.7\,\text{litres}}{25\,\text{ml}} = \frac{1.7 \times 1000\,\text{ml}}{25\,\text{ml}} = 68$$

Do It Yourself

1 a Change to kilograms:

(i) 7431 g   (ii) 376 100 mg   (iii) 4.5 t

b A security firm delivers £100 worth of 1 pence pieces to a supermarket. Calculate the weight of these coins, in kilograms, if each coin weighs 3.45 g.

c Write in order of size, smallest first:

70 g   0.7 kg   700 mg   0.7 mg

d Twenty-four tins of meat are packed into a carton and the total weight is 16 kg. If the carton alone weighs 400 g, calculate the weight of one tin of meat.

'The metric system is based around dividing and multiplying by tens'

e A caterer uses 400 g of potatoes per day for each person. Find the cost of providing for 55 people for 5 days with the potatoes costing 27p per kilogram.

f A ream of paper (500 sheets) weighs 3 kg. What is the weight, in grams, of one sheet? If the pile is 7 cm thick, what is the thickness of one sheet in millimetres?

2 a Convert to millimetres:

    (i) 4.6 cm   (ii) 7.9 cm   (iii) 9.1 m   (iv) 31.2 m

b Convert to centimetres:

    (i) 5 m   (ii) 9.2 m   (iii) 740 mm   (iv) 6431 mm

c Convert to kilometres:

    (i) 800 m   (ii) 400 cm   (iii) 650 mm   (iv) 21 m

3 Cough mixture is sold in bottles containing 5 fl oz. If 1 fl oz = 28.41 ml, work out to the nearest centilitre the amount, in centilitres, that should be put on the bottle label.

Statistics and Probability

Things You Need to Know

1 In mathematics the word **average** simply means a central value that represents the set of values. The average is used as a representative of the whole collection of values. There are three main types of average – the **mean**, the **mode** and the **median**.

$$\text{Mean} = \frac{\text{total of the values in the list}}{\text{number of values in the list}}$$

(can only be used when the items are numbers)

Median – the middle value when the values are arranged in order
(or halfway between the middle two values)

Mode – the value that occurs the most often
(can be used with any sort of data – numeric or non-numeric)

2 If there are a lot of data they are best summarised in a **frequency table**, which tells us how many times each value has occurred.

Sometimes even this is not very useful (particularly if the range of values is quite large and there are possible values that are not used); in this case we group the values into class intervals. The resulting table is known as a

'A jumble of figures is called raw data'

grouped frequency table. For example, here is a list of marks 50 pupils received in a science examination. For these data it makes sense to group the values as shown in the following grouped frequency table.

80	93	63	74	51	60	61	54	69	54
51	44	33	70	40	30	55	57	59	55
4	51	46	47	56	58	62	33	45	48
37	56	39	51	14	43	47	58	39	42
66	63	65	71	23	26	81	65	77	68

Mark group	Mid-value	Frequency	Freq. × mid-value
0–9	4.5	1	4.5
10–19	14.5	1	14.5
20–29	24.5	2	49
30–39	34.5	6	207
40–49	44.5	9	400.5
50–59	55.5	14	777
60–69	65.5	10	655
70–70	75.5	4	302
80–89	85.5	2	171
90–99	95.5	1	95.5
		50	2676

The table provides a useful way to estimate the mean, using the mid-value of each group, and assuming that this is the value of each value in that group. (Some will be higher and some lower, but it should more or less even out.) To estimate the **mean**, you divide the total of the mid-values by the number of entries. So, in our example,

$$\text{mean} = \frac{\text{total of mid-values}}{\text{number of entries}} = \frac{2676}{50} = 53.52$$

(Compare this figure with the mean obtained using the individual figures: 52.68.)

3 A **frequency diagram** is used to represent a frequency table; it has frequency on the vertical axis. When you draw a frequency diagram don't forget to label the axes and put a title. The frequency diagram given here shows the data from the above example.

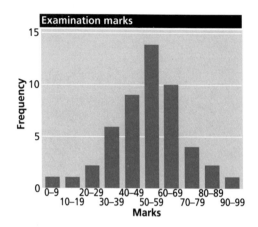

    The grouped frequency table can be made into a cumulative frequency table, by the addition of another column. This provides a running total of the frequency. In the preceding chart, the cumulative frequency column would read 1, 2, 4, 10, 19, 33, 43, 47, 49, 50.

    These data are then used to draw a **cumulative frequency graph**. The cumulative frequency is always put on the vertical scale, and the *top* value for that group on the horizontal scale. The graph usually forms a characteristic 'S' shape as shown here.

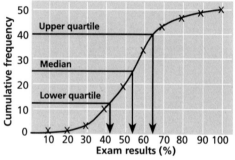

    From this, useful statistics can be found. Reading across from the point halfway up the vertical scale gives the **median** on the horizontal scale, while reading across from the points one-quarter and three-quarters of the way up the scale gives the **lower quartile (LQ)** and **upper quartile (UQ)** respectively. The **interquartile range** is the difference between the upper quartile and the lower quartile. The cumulative frequency graph for the science examination example is shown here.

4 The **modal class** is the same sort of thing as the mode – it is the class with the most members in a grouped frequency table. The modal class is shown as the highest bar on a frequency diagram – don't forget that it covers a range of values, *not* a single value, and it may not even contain the actual modal value. For our example the modal class is 50–59.

5 A **pie chart** gives an alternative way of displaying information. A pie chart is a circle divided up into segments, each segment representing a value (or group of values) and the angle of the segment being the frequency.

Remember there are 360° in the circle and so the angle for each segment is

$$\text{Angle of segment} = \frac{\text{number in group}}{\text{total number}} \times 360°$$

Again, don't forget to put a title and also label the segments.

The pie chart on the right shows the results of a survey of favourite colours in which each of the six colours was equally popular.

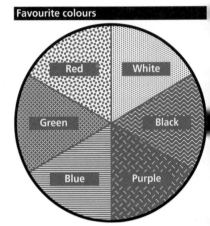

Favourite colours

6   We can use graphs in the form of **conversion graphs** to change from one scale of values to another scale – e.g. kilometres and miles, using the fact that 8 km = 5 miles.

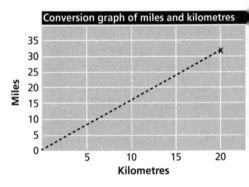

Conversion graph of miles and kilometres

The main point about using a conversion graph is that it literally 'does the calculation' for you – just by plotting two points and joining them. In the example above, the two points are (0, 0) and (20, 32), as 0 miles is 0 km and 20 miles is 32 km.

7   **Scatter diagrams** are used to see if there is a connection between two sets of values – e.g. is there a connection between height and weight?

Height (cm)	165	168	170	170	173	180	183	185	188	190
Weight (kg)	65.8	63.6	76.2	73.4	68.1	77.0	65.6	69.6	78.5	81.7

From the graph it does look as if there is a connection – the taller a person is the more they weigh – but there is not a sufficiently good connection to be able to predict with any accuracy a person's weight given their height, or their height given their weight.

Height (cm) and weight (kg) of 10 men

3 **Probability** is simply a way of assessing how likely something is to happen. A scale from 0 to 1 is used for it, with fractional or decimal values in between. In other words, if an event is bound to happen, the probability is 1, e.g. tossing a head with a double-headed coin. If an event will never happen the probability is 0, e.g. your maths teacher going to the moon.

One way of finding the probability is

$$\text{Probability of event happening} = \frac{\text{number of ways the event can happen}}{\text{number of possible outcomes}}$$

This also means that we could use probability to predict how many times something is likely to happen.

When we have two events (say, A and B) which are independent we can calculate the probabilities using the following connection. If Pr(A) represents the probability of event A happening and Pr(B) the probability of event B happening, then

$$\text{Pr}(A \text{ or } B) = \text{Pr}(A) + \text{Pr}(B)$$
$$\text{Pr}(A \text{ and } B) = \text{Pr}(A) \times \text{Pr}(B)$$

Sometimes it is easier to draw a diagram all the possible outcomes. The best type of diagram is a **tree diagram**. Here is a tree diagram representing the spinning of a three-sided spinner (with different coloured sides, red (R), green (G) and blue (B)). It is spun three times.

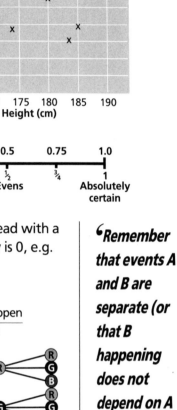

'Remember that events A and B are separate (or that B happening does not depend on A happening)'

'What you must be sure of is whether you add the probabilities or multiply them'

65

The tree diagram shows all the possible results of spinning the spinner, each of which is equally likely to happen. If the top line of the tree is followed, we can see that this gives RRR or 3 reds. If we follow the lines to the top asterisked point this gives RGB in that order. The asterisked points are those where the outcome is one of each colour.

The tree diagram shows that there are 27 possible outcomes. Since there are 6 ways that we can get each colour once (as shown by the asterisks), the probability of getting one of each colour is:

$$\frac{6}{27} = \frac{2}{9}$$

How to Do It

1 The school hockey team scored the following number of goals in 10 matches:

2   3   1   0   3   1   5   2   0   1

Find:

(i) the mean number of goals scored per match;
(ii) the median number of goals scored;
(iii) the modal number of goals scored.

Solution

(i) Mean $= (2+3+1+0+3+1+5+2+0+1) \div 10$
     $= 1.8$ goals per match

(ii) For the median, arrange the values in order:

0   0   1   1   1   2   2   3   3   5

The median score is between 1 and 2, so the median is

$(1+2) \div 2 = 1.5$

(iii) The mode, the most common score, is 1 goal.

2 The shoe sizes of 32 members of a club are

```
8   10   6   7   7   8   9   8
7    7   6   7   5   8   7   7
6    9   7   8   6   7   8   5
7    8   7   5   8   6   7   9
```

Produce a frequency table and find the mode.

Solution

	Tally	Frequency
5	III	3
6	IIII	5
7	IIII IIII II	12
8	IIII III	8
9	III	3
10	I	1
	Total	32

Mode = size 7.

Size	5	6	7	8	9	10
Frequency	3	5	12	8	3	1

3 Draw a frequency diagram for the information in question 2.

Solution
The highest frequency is 12 so
we need to choose a vertical
scale to cope with this:

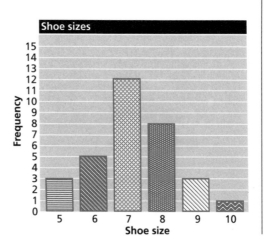

*'Note how
the modal
value is the
highest bar'*

67

4 a In a survey, 150 people were asked to select a number between 1 and 100. Here is a grouped frequency table showing the results:

Group	1–10	11–20	21–30	31–40	41–50	51–60	61–70	71–80	81–90	91–100
Frequency	18	14	16	14	13	20	9	14	25	7

(i) What is the modal class?

(ii) What is the modal class if the groups are 1–20, 21–40 and so on?

Solution

(i) The modal class is 81–90 (typical value 85.5).

(ii) If grouped in 20s we get

Group	1–20	21–40	41–60	61–80	81–100
Frequency	32	30	33	23	32

The modal class is now 41–60 (but there is now not much difference between most of them).

b A football club has two teams, called Red and Yellow, in the same league. The goals scored by each team in the 30 matches they played in a season are summarised in the table:

Goals	0	1	2	3	4	5	6	7
Red	5	4	7	9	3	1	0	1
Yellow	6	3	4	7	5	3	1	1

In order to decide which is the better team, find the mean and mode of the number of goals scored by each team. Which team is better?

Solution

Red team:

The modal number of goals scored is 3.

The mean is:

$$\frac{5\times0+4\times1+7\times2+9\times3+3\times4+1\times5+0\times6+1\times7}{5+4+7+9+3+1+0+1}$$

$$=\frac{0+4+14+27+12+5+0+7}{30}$$

$$=\frac{69}{30}$$

$$=2.3$$

Yellow team:

The modal number of goals scored is 3.

The mean is:

$$\frac{6\times0+3\times1+4\times2+7\times3+5\times4+3\times5+1\times6+1\times7}{6+3+4+7+5+3+1+1}$$

$$=\frac{0+3+8+21+20+15+6+7}{30}$$

$$=\frac{80}{30}$$

$$=2.7$$

Thus, although both teams have the same modal number of goals scored, the Yellow team have a higher mean (despite having more matches where they failed to score). So on this evidence the Yellow team is better than the Red team.

5 **a** The pie chart shows how 160 men travel from home to the factory where they work. How many men travel by train?

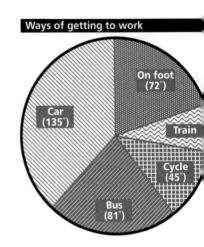

Ways of getting to work

Solution
Since all the angles should total 360°, the angle for 'train' is

$$360° - (72° + 135° + 81° + 45°) = 27°$$

360° represents 160 people, so 27° represents

$$\frac{160}{360} \times 27 = 12 \text{ people}$$

b The sales in a baker's shop for one week were

> White bread   £160
> Wholemeal bread   £140
> Cakes   £100
> Flour   £52
> Biscuits   £28

Draw a pie chart to represent this information.

Solution
Total sales = £480, so the angle for 'white bread' is

$$\frac{160}{480} \times 360 = 120°$$

Similar calculations for the others give

> Wholemeal bread 105°   Cakes 75°   Flour 39°   Biscuits 21°

The pie chart is shown on the right.

A baker's shop sales

6 A farmer has 900 acres of land. In the metric system this would be measured in hectares (10 000 m²). If 1 acre is approximately 4047 m² how many hectares of land does the farmer have?

Solution

We know that 1 acre = .405 hectares, so we can plot the points for 100 acres = 405 hectares and 0 acres = 0 hectares, then draw a line between them. Here is the conversion graph:

From the graph 900 acres = about 360 hectares. (A larger, more detailed graph would give the more precise answer of 364 hectares.)

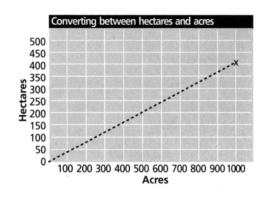

7 Twelve pupils were to take two mathematics test papers. Unfortunately, one was absent for the first paper and another was absent for the second. Here are the marks for the pupils:

Pupil	A	B	C	D	E	F	G	H	J	K	L	M
Paper 1	77	52	62	44	50	53	abs	68	71	60	38	59
Paper 2	76	49	abs	34	39	44	36	66	68	60	24	50

Plot a scatter diagram for the results where both marks are known. By drawing a line that 'fits' the points (known as a **line of 'best fit'**) give estimates of the likely marks for the two absent pupils.

Solution

Candidate C got 62 on paper 1 and an estimated 55 on paper 2.
Candidate G got 36 on paper 2 and an estimated 42 on paper 1.

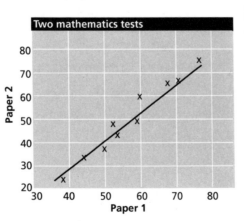

'To draw a line of best fit, use your judgement to line up the ruler so that half of the crosses are above it and half below'

8 **a** Ten counters have the numbers 1 to 10 printed on them. They are placed in a bag and one is picked out. What is the probability that the number on the counter is

(i) odd   (ii) a multiple of 3   (iii) a prime number?

Solution

(i) The odd numbers from 1 to 10 are

1   3   5   7   9   (5 of them)

so $\text{Pr(odd)} = \dfrac{5}{10}$. The probability of it being odd $= \dfrac{1}{2}$ or 0.5   (some would write 50%).

(ii) The multiples of 3 are

3   6   9   (3 of them)

The probability of a multiple of 3 $= \dfrac{3}{10} = 0.3$.

(iii) The prime numbers are

2   3   5   7   (4 of them)

The probability of a prime $= \dfrac{4}{10} = 0.4$.

b A box contains 7 red and 12 yellow counters. Two are selected. What is the probability that they are both yellow?

Solution

As there are 19 counters in total and 12 of them are yellow, then the probability of drawing a yellow counter on the first selection is

$\dfrac{12}{19}$

We could summarise this as

$\text{Pr}(Y_1) = \dfrac{12}{19}$ (where Y means yellow and the $_1$ means the first selection)

When the second selection is made we assume that the first was successful – i.e. a yellow was selected. This means that there are now only 18 counters to select from and of these only 11 are yellow. (If the first selection had not been a yellow, there would be no point in going on with selecting.)

As there are 18 counters now and 11 of them are yellow, then the probability of drawing a yellow counter on the first selection is

$$\frac{11}{18}$$

We could summarise this as:

$Pr(Y_2) = \frac{11}{18}$ (where Y means yellow and the $_2$ means the second selection)

So, we get

$$Pr(Y_1 \text{ and } Y_2) = Pr(Y_1) \times Pr(Y_2)$$
$$= \frac{12}{19} \times \frac{11}{18} = \frac{22}{57}$$

We could draw a tree diagram of the situation with the probabilities on the branches, instead of each branch being equally likely:

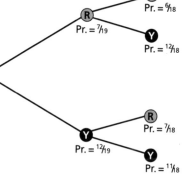

In the diagram you will note that for each pair of branches coming from a point the total of the probabilities is 1 – because one or other of them *must* happen.

Now we could proceed as before:

$$Pr(Y_1 \text{ and } Y_2) = Pr(Y_1) \times Pr(Y_2)$$
$$= \frac{12}{19} \times \frac{11}{18} = \frac{22}{57}$$

9 A bag contains three red and two green fruit-drops. Draw a tree diagram to show the result of taking one sweet then a second, without replacing the first sweet. What is the probability of:

(i) two red;

(ii) two green;

(iii) one of each.

Solution

Each pathway in this tree is equally likely, with the first set of branches being the first choice and the second set each time representing a further choice from what remains. So we have 20 possible outcomes, all equally likely.

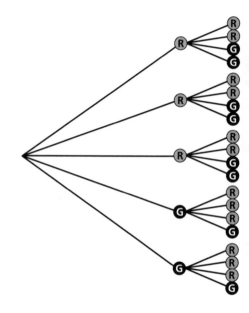

(i) Of the 20 outcomes 6 have two reds so the probability of 2 reds is

$$\tfrac{6}{20} = 0.3$$

(ii) Of the 20 outcomes 2 have two greens so the probability of 2 greens is

$$\tfrac{2}{20} = 0.1$$

(iii) Of the 20 outcomes 12 are one of each so the probability of one of each is

$$\tfrac{12}{20} = 0.6$$

Do It Yourself

1 a The heights of nine girls (in centimetres) are

169   162   171   166   162   178   179   169   162

Find:

    (i) the mean height;
    (ii) the median height;
    (iii) the modal height.

b The number of goals scored by a football team in 12 consecutive matches were:

    1 1 4 0 0 2 5 3 0 2 6 0

Find:
- (i) the mean number of goals,
- (ii) the median number and
- (iii) the modal number of goals.

2 The number of words in each line of a page of *Journey to the Centre of the Earth* by Jules Verne are shown below. Form a frequency table.

   9 8 6   8 5 9   1 10   9 10
  10 8 1   1 3 6   6 10 12   3
   8 3 9 12 2 8 11 10   9 11

3a Draw a frequency diagram of the results in Question 2.

b The frequency table below shows the number of pints of milk delivered on one day to the houses in Lime Avenue:

No. of pints delivered	0	1	2	3	4	5
Frequency	15	32	13	10	2	1

- (i) Draw a frequency diagram to illustrate these data.
- (ii) How many houses are there in Lime Avenue?
- (iii) How many houses received just one pint of milk on the day in question?
- (iv) How many pints of milk were delivered to Lime Avenue?

4 Here are the marks for 40 pupils. Form a grouped frequency table using intervals of 5 marks (1–5, 6–10, 11–15, etc.). What is the modal class?

  20 19 18   6 25 15 16 30 17 25   2 22   5 22 23   8
  15   7   6 12 13 26 21 12 14 28   9 18 13 19 16 31
  38 20 33 10 42 16 47 13

5 a A survey was done on 360 people to find out what they used to heat their houses. The results are shown here. Draw a pie chart to illustrate these data.

Fuel	Number of houses
Coal	40
Electricity	80
Gas	145
Oil	95

b Company sales

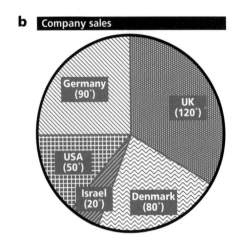

This pie chart shows the sales figures of a company in various countries. If the sales in the UK amounted to £2 700 000 find the total sales figures for each of the other countries.

'It's worth checking that all the segments add up to 360° now, before you draw it out'

c In 1994, 35% of the assets of a company were in Switzerland, 30% in the UK, 20% in North America and the rest were elsewhere. Draw a pie chart to illustrate these data.

6 There are approximately 2.2 lb in 1 kg. Draw a conversion graph for this with scales from 0 to 30 for the pound scale. Using the conversion graph find the weight in kilograms of 15 lb and the weight in pounds which is equivalent to 8 kg.

7 A group of eight language students were given tests in French and German:

Pupil	1	2	3	4	5	6	7	8
French	10	31	37	11	26	18	15	22
German	9	34	35	15	26	20	14	21

Draw a scatter diagram and on it draw the line of 'best fit'.

If another pupil only did the French test and scored 17, what mark would you estimate for his or her German mark?

8a In a vehicle park there are 100 vehicles – 85 are cars, 10 are lorries and 5 are buses. If they are all equally likely to leave, what is the probability that:

(i) a bus leaves first;

(ii) a car leaves after a bus has left first.

b Two unbiased dice, one red and the other blue, are used in a game. The red dice is marked 1 1 1 2 2 3 and the blue dice is marked 1 2 3 3 5 5. Complete the following table showing the possible sums of the two dice:

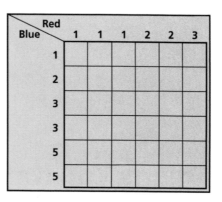

Blue \ Red	1	1	1	2	2	3
1						
2						
3						
3						
5						
5						

(i) What is the probability of getting a score of 6?

(ii) What is the probability of the two dice showing the same result?

(iii) At the end of the game Trish needs 4 and Neeva needs 5. Who is more likely to win and why?

9a A bag contains six 20p coins and three 50p coins. Two coins are selected at random. Draw a tree diagram to illustrate this and use it to find the probability that:

(i) both coins are 20p coins;

(ii) both coins are 50p coins;

(iii) the first is a 20p coin and the second is a 50p coin;

(iv) there is exactly one 20p coin.

b A coin is spun three times. Draw a tree diagram to illustrate all the possible results. Find the probability of getting

(i) three heads;

(ii) two heads and a tail in any order.

9 | Graphs

Things You Need to Know

1 The position of a point on a graph is given by its **coordinates**. The coordinate is a measure of how far along and up or down the point is from some fixed origin. Here are some points:

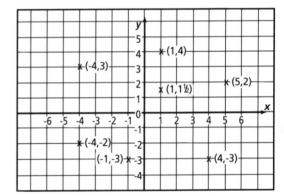

2 The **gradient** is found by drawing a right-angled triangle using the straight line as the hypotenuse and lines parallel to the x- and y-axes to form the right angle.

In the graph shown on the right

$$\text{Gradient} = \frac{\text{Change in } y\text{-values}}{\text{Change in } x\text{-values}}$$

$$= \frac{9}{3} = 3$$

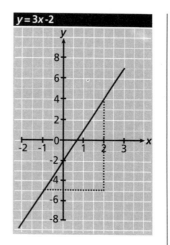

3 The equation of a **straight line graph** can always be written in the form

$$y = mx + c$$

where m is the gradient and c the point where it crosses the y-axis (the y-axis intercept).

    Remember that if the gradient is *positive* the line slopes *upwards* when going left to right; if the gradient is *negative* it slopes *downwards* when going left to right; if the gradient is 0 the line is horizontal.

'The slope of a line is called its gradient'

4 When drawing a graph *always* draw a **table of values** to produce the y-value from the x-value. For the graph above ($y = 3x - 2$) the table is:

x	-2	-1	0	1	2	3
$3x$	-6	-3	0	3	6	9
-2	-2	-2	-2	-2	-2	-2
y	-8	-5	-2	1	4	7

Equations like

$$y = x^2 + 1$$

produce curves for their graphs, not a series of straight lines.

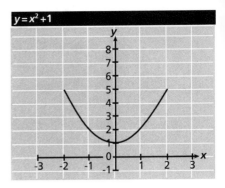
$y = x^2 + 1$

x	-2	-1	0	1	2
x^2	4	1	0	1	4
$+1$	$+1$	$+1$	$+1$	$+1$	$+1$
y	5	2	1	2	5

All graphs with the highest power of x being 2 will have a shape like the one above – it is called a **parabola**.

We can also get curves for equations like

$$y = \frac{24}{x}$$

Here is its table of values and graph:

x	-12	-8	-6	-4	-3	-2	-1	1	2	3	4	6	8	12
y	-2	-3	-4	-6	-8	-12	-24	24	12	8	6	4	3	2

A curve like this is called a **hyperbola**.

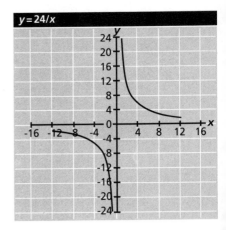
$y = 24/x$

'Note that no value is given for $x = 0$, the reason being that there isn't one! Dividing by 0 is not allowed'

How to Do It

1 Plot these points and join them within their groups.
  (i) $(1, 4\frac{1}{2})$ $(3\frac{1}{2}, 1)$ $(\frac{1}{2}, 1)$ (ii) $(-\frac{1}{2}, 4)$ $(-\frac{1}{2}, 1)$ $(-2\frac{1}{2}, 1)$
  (iii) $(4, 0)$ $(3\frac{1}{2}, -\frac{1}{2})$ $(-2\frac{1}{2}, -\frac{1}{2})$ $(-3, \frac{1}{2})$

Solution

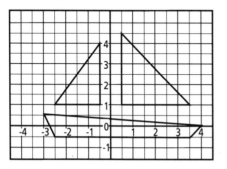

'The first coordinate value is how far across and the second is how far up – x goes across and y goes up'

2 For each of the following pairs of points find the gradient of the line joining them: (i) $(0, 0)$ and $(3, 6)$ (ii) $(2, 4)$ and $(5, 1)$ (iii) $(-3, -2)$ and $(9, 4)$

Solution
One way would be to draw each of them on squared paper, but really they are all very similar, so you only need one diagram, as shown on the right. We can see that the difference between the x-values gives the horizontal distance and the difference between the y-values gives the vertical distance. Then it is easy to find the gradient.

(i) Horizontal distance $= 3 - 0 = 3$
    Vertical distance $= 6 - 0 = 6$
        Gradient $= 6 \div 3 = 2$

(ii) Horizontal distance $= 5 - 2 = 3$
     Vertical distance $= 1 - 4 = -3$ (careful here – get it the right way round!)
        Gradient $= -3 \div 3 = -1$

(iii) Horizontal distance $= 9 - -3 = 9 + 3 = 12$
      Vertical distance $= 4 - -2 = 4 + 2 = 6$

        Gradient $= 6 \div 12 = \dfrac{1}{2}$

3 **a** The following equations represent straight line graphs. In each case find the gradient and the y-axis intercept without drawing the graph.

    (i) $y = 3x - 5$ (ii) $3y = 6x - 2$

    (iii) $5y = 2x + 10$ (iv) $2x + 3y = 5$

Solution

    (i) For $y = 3x - 5$, the gradient $= 3$ and the y-axis intercept $= -5$.

    (ii) For $3y = 6x - 2$, this becomes

$$y = 2x - \frac{2}{3} \quad \text{(dividing by 3)}$$

so the gradient $= 2$ and the y-axis intercept $= -\frac{2}{3}$.

    (iii) For $5y = 2x + 10$, this becomes

$$y = \frac{2}{5}x + 2 \quad \text{(dividing by 5)}$$

so the gradient $= \frac{2}{5}$ and the y-axis intercept $= 2$.

    (iv) For $2x + 3y = 5$, this becomes

$$3y = -2x + 5 \quad \text{(isolating } y\text{)}$$

$$y = \frac{-2}{3}x + \frac{5}{3} \quad \text{(dividing by 3)}$$

so the gradient $= -\frac{2}{3}$ and the y-axis intercept $= \frac{5}{3}$.

b What is the equation of each of these straight line graphs (draw a sketch):

    (i) gradient $= 2$, y-axis intercept $= -1$;

    (ii) gradient $= \frac{3}{5}$, y-axis intercept $= 1$;

    (iii) gradient $= \frac{4}{3}$, y-axis intercept $= \frac{1}{3}$.

Solution

(i) $y = 2x - 1$

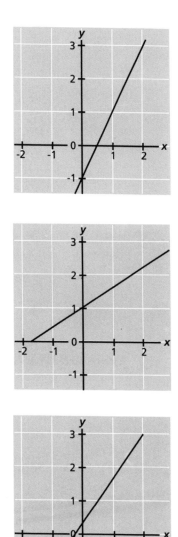

(ii) $5y = 3x + 5$

(iii) $3y = 4x + 1$

c Here are some points that are on a straight line graph. Plot the points and draw the straight line to find the equation of the line.

x	2	4	6	8	10	12
y	10	16	22	28	34	40

Solution

The *y*-axis intercept is 4 and the gradient is 3, so

$$y = 3x + 4$$

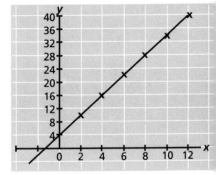

d During an experiment to verify Ohm's law the following results were obtained:

E(volts)	0	1.0	2.0	2.5	3.7	4.1	5.9	6.8	8.0
I(amps)	0	0.24	0.5	0.63	0.92	1.05	1.48	1.70	2.05

> **'Strictly speaking if we spot that it is a straight line we only really need to plot three points'**

Draw the best straight line through the points and find its equation.

Solution

The *y*-axis intercept is 0 and the gradient is $\frac{1}{4}$, so

$$I = \frac{1}{4}E$$

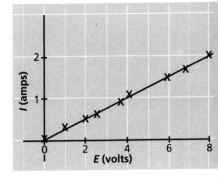

e Draw the graph of $y = 2x - 5$ for values of *x* between -3 and 4. Use the graph to find the solution of $2x - 5 = 2$.

Solution

First you need to produce a table of values:

x	-3	-2	-1	0	1	2	3	4
$2x$	-6	-4	-2	0	2	4	6	8
-5	-5	-5	-5	-5	-5	-5	-5	-5
y	-11	-9	-7	-5	-3	-1	1	3

$$y = 2x - 5$$

$2x - 5 = 2$ is when $y = 2$, so

$$x = 3\frac{1}{2}$$

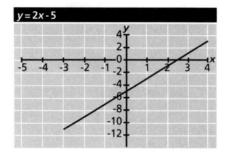

4 Draw the graph of the equation $y = 2x^2 - x - 6$ for values of x between -4 and 6. Hence solve the equations:

(i) $2x^2 - x - 6 = 0$ (ii) $2x^2 - x - 4 = 0$ (iii) $2x^2 - x - 9 = 0$

Solution

First produce a table of values:

x	-4	-3	-2	-1	0	1	2	3	4	5	6
$2x^2$	32	18	8	2	0	2	8	18	32	50	72
$-x$	4	3	2	1	0	-1	-2	-3	-4	-5	-6
-6	-6	-6	-6	-6	-6	-6	-6	-6	-6	-6	-6
y	30	15	4	-3	-6	-5	0	9	22	39	60

'When you draw a line graph that is not a straight line always twist the graph paper round so that your hand is inside the curve – it will help you get a smoother curve'

Now plot the points and draw the graph. (You will need a larger, more precise graph than the one shown here.)

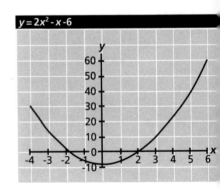

$y = 2x^2 - x - 6$

(i) On the graph when $y = 0$, $2x^2 - x - 6 = 0$, so

$x = -1.5$ or 2

(ii) $2x^2 - x - 4 = 0$ is when $y = -2$ for $y = 2x^2 - x - 6$, so

$x = -1.2$ or 1.7

(iii) $2x^2 - x - 9 = 0$ is when $y = 3$ for $y = 2x^2 - x - 6$, so

$x = -1.9$ or 2.4

(You should note that these are approximate answers.)

Do It Yourself

'Coordinates can be thought of as an address'

1 Plot these points in the groups given:

(i) $(4, 3\frac{1}{2})$, $(4, -1)$, $(1\frac{1}{2}, -1)$, $(1\frac{1}{2}, 3\frac{1}{2})$
(ii) $(3\frac{1}{2}, 3)$, $(3\frac{1}{2}, 1\frac{1}{2})$, $(2, 1\frac{1}{2})$, $(2\frac{1}{2}, 3)$
(iii) $(1, 2)$, $(1, -1)$, $(-4, -1)$, $(-4, 2)$
(iv) $(-3, 3\frac{1}{2})$, $(-3, 4\frac{1}{2})$, $(-3\frac{1}{2}, 4\frac{1}{2})$, $(-3\frac{1}{2}, 3\frac{1}{2})$
(v) $(-2\frac{1}{2}, -1\frac{1}{2})$, $(-2, -2)$, $(-2\frac{1}{2}, -2\frac{1}{2})$, $(-3, -2)$
(join the points above with a curve)
(vi) $(3, -1\frac{1}{2})$, $(3\frac{1}{2}, -2)$, $(3, -2\frac{1}{2})$, $(2\frac{1}{2}, -2)$
(join the points above with a curve)

2a The points A and B have coordinates $(-1, -4)$ and $(4, 1)$ respectively.

(i) Find the gradient of AB.
(ii) Calculate the length of A, using Pythagoras' theorem (see page 105).

b On squared paper and using the same scale for the x-axis and for the y-axis draw a line from the point $(0, 0)$ to the point $(8, 6)$. Through the point $(4, 3)$ draw a line at right angles to the original line.

(i) Find the gradient of each of the lines.

(ii) What value do you get when you multiply the values of the gradients?

'Choose a
scale which
uses as much
of your piece
of paper as
possible'

3a For each of the graphs below find the gradient of the line and the y-axis intercept.

(i) $y = 4x - 7$ (ii) $y = 2x + 9$ (iii) $y = 6x + 3$

(iv) $y = 5x - \dfrac{1}{2}$ (v) $y = \dfrac{1}{4}x - 2$ (vi) $y = 8 - x$

b Find the equation of the straight line given the gradient and y-axis intercept.

	Gradient	y-axis intercept		Gradient	y-axis intercept
(i)	3	4	(iv)	4	-6
(ii)	-2	-2			
(iii)	$-\dfrac{1}{2}$	3	(v)	-1	$-\dfrac{1}{4}$

4a (i) Copy and complete the following table for values of x between -4 and 4:

x	-4	-3	-2	-1	0	1	2	3	4
x^2	16				0	1			

(ii) Draw the graph of $y = x^2$, for x-values between -4 and 4. Use your graph to find the square of 1.8 and the square root of 13.

b Draw the graph of $y = x^2$ and $y = 2x + 1$ for values of x from -1 to $+3$. From the graph read the solutions to the equation

$$x^2 - 2x - 1 = 0$$

c Sketch the graph of $y = x^2 - 4x - 5$ for $-2 \leqslant x \leqslant 4$, showing clearly its axis of symmetry. (See Section 14 for more about axes of symmetry.)

'Don't forget
to label the
axes of any
graph and put
a title'

10 Time, Speed and Travel Graphs

Things You Need to Know

1 **Time**: 60 seconds = 1 minute, 60 minutes = 1 hour, 24 hours = 1 day. These are all basic facts that we live with but we also need to be able to switch easily between using the 12-hour clock with a.m. and p.m. to indicate before and after noon, and the 24-hour clock. Here are some sample times throughout a day written in both systems:

12-hour	24-hour	12-hour	24-hour	12-hour	24-hour
12.15 a.m.	00.15	12.00 noon	12.00	8.00 p.m.	20.00
7.05 a.m.	07.05	2.15 p.m.	14.15	11.10 p.m.	23.10
10.20 a.m.	10.20	6.35 p.m.	18.35	midnight	00.00

2 Whenever we are moving, the time it takes to move from start to finish, depends upon two things – how far we move and how fast we travel. We define **average speed** in the following way:

$$\text{Average speed} = \frac{\text{total distance travelled}}{\text{total time taken}}$$

The formula can also be re-arranged:

$$\text{Total time taken} = \frac{\text{total distance travelled}}{\text{average speed}}$$

The units are based upon the units in which the distance was measured (miles, kilometres, feet, metres, etc.) and the units of time (second, minute, hour, etc.). It can be written as, for example, 5 km per hr, 5 kph, 5 km/hr or 5 km hr^{-1}.

3 Average speed does not give a clear picture – it is a summary, and like all summaries the detail is missing. One way of showing what is happening is with a **travel graph** showing how the distance from your starting point is changing. On the right is a **distance-time graph** of Gary taking his dog for a walk:

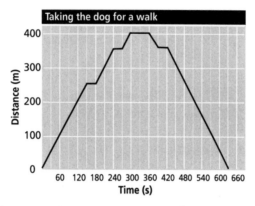

Here the distance (in metres) is on the vertical scale and the time (in seconds) is on the horizontal scale – so Gary only took his dog for a walk for 10½ minutes (630 seconds). We can see that they stopped four times. The steepness (gradient) of each of the lines gives the speed – the faster they travel the steeper the line. When it is horizontal they are stopped.

How to Do It

1 Write the following times in the other system (i.e. if it is in 12-hour clock form write it in 24-hour form and if it is in 24-hour form write it in 12-hour form):

    (i) 9.55 a.m.   (ii) 05.37   (iii) 14.14   (iv) 12.15 a.m.

Solution

  (i) 9.55 a.m. is 09.55   (ii) 05.37 is 5.37 a.m.

  (iii) 14.14 is 2.14 p.m.   (iv) 12.15 a.m. is 00.15

2^a This time, Gary took his dog for a 3 km walk, which took him 45 minutes. What was their speed:

  (i) in kilometres/minute;   (ii) in kilometres/hour.

We are not worried about how he slowed down and speeded up, just that it took 45 minutes to travel 3 km.

'Any time after 1.00 p.m. is written with a 12 added to the hours in the 24-hour system'

89

Solution

(i) Average speed $= \dfrac{3\,km}{45\,minutes}$

$= \dfrac{1}{15}\,km/min$

$= 0.061\,km/min$

(ii) His speed in kilometres/hour is

$60 \times \dfrac{1}{15} = 4\,km/h$

b A vehicle travels 300 km in 5 hours. Calculate its average speed.

Solution

Average speed $= \dfrac{300\,km}{5\,hours}$

$= 60\,km/h$

c A car travels 400 km at an average speed of 80 km/h. How long does the journey take?

Solution

Time taken $= \dfrac{400\,km}{8\,km/hr}$

$= 5\,hours$

3 A train left London going to Newcastle (420 km) at 13.00 hours. It stopped at Grantham (180 km from London) for 15 minutes. It stopped again at York (315 km from London) for 15 minutes. Except for when it stopped, it travelled at a steady 70 km/h.

(i) Draw a distance–time graph for the train journey.
(ii) What time did the train reach Newcastle?

Solution

In order to answer this we have to first think about the scales – we know that the distance scale has to go to 420 km, and since 70 divides into 420 six times our time must cover from 13.00 to more than 19.00, so let's take it to 20.00.

Start at (13.00, 0) and draw a line that indicates 70 km/h by drawing through the point (15.00, 140), i.e. 2 hours later. Now extend this line. Find where the line indicates that 180 km has been covered (i.e. at Grantham); here, draw a line horizontally for 15 minutes to indicate it stopped for this time. Now draw a line from this point parallel to the first. Find at what point it has covered 315 km (i.e. at York) and draw a horizontal line for 15 minutes. Last, from this point draw a line parallel to the first until you reach 420 km from London (i.e. the train has arrived at Newcastle).

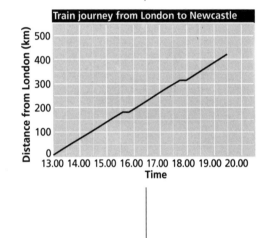

    From the graph it reached Newcastle at 19.30 (or 7.30 p.m.).

Do It Yourself

1 a A man sets his video recorder to record some programmes. He has to tell his recorder the start and finish times. In the table on the right, the three columns represent the start time, the finish time and the length of the programme in hours and minutes. Copy the table and fill in the gaps.

b Rewrite the table in question 1a using the 12-hour clock.

Start time	Finish time	Length
08.00	08.40	0h 40m
14.15	?	1h 10m
?	17.40	0h 50m
19.30	21.00	?
11.40	?	2h 25m

2a A coach leaves Bristol at 09.45 to travel to Aberdeen, 480 miles away. The journey takes 8 hours and 20 minutes. What time does the coach arrive in Aberdeen, and what was its average speed?

b Mark left home at 6.30 a.m. to travel to the airport 115 miles away. He travelled the first 15 miles at an average speed of 45 miles/hour and the rest at an average of 40 miles/hour.

(i) At what time did he arrive, assuming he did not stop on the way?
(ii) What was his average speed for the whole journey?

c Vicky runs for $1\frac{1}{2}$ hours at 12 km/h and then for 1 hour at 15 km/h and then finally for $\frac{1}{2}$ hour at 10 km/h.

(i) How far does she run altogether?
(ii) The next day she runs the same distance at a constant speed in the same time. What is this speed?

3 The graph shows Philip's journey from home to school. He walked to the bus stop, waited and then caught the bus to school.

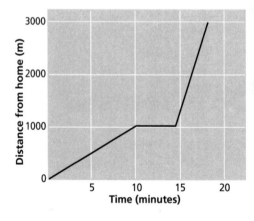

(i) How long did it take him to walk to the bus stop?
(ii) How long did he wait at the bus stop?
(iii) How far from home was he after 13 minutes?
(iv) How far is it from the bus stop to school?

Angles and Loci

Things You Need to Know

1 The following basic facts about angles:
  (i) The angles on a straight line total 180°.

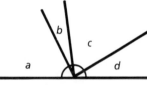

$$a + b + c + d = 180°$$

  (ii) The angles round a point total 360°.

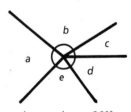

$$a + b + c + d + e = 360°$$

(iii) The use of the names **acute** (less than 90°), **right angle** (equal to 90°), **obtuse** (greater than 90° and less than 180°) and **reflex** (greater than 180°).

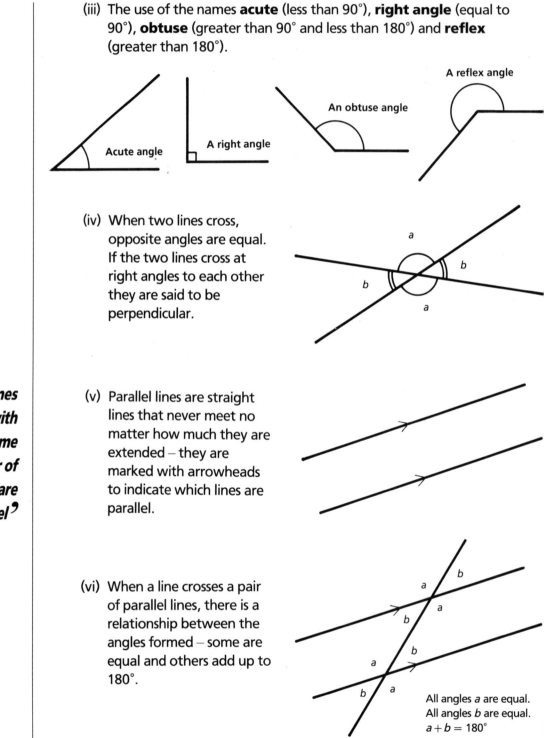

Acute angle

A right angle

An obtuse angle

A reflex angle

(iv) When two lines cross, opposite angles are equal. If the two lines cross at right angles to each other they are said to be perpendicular.

'All lines marked with the same number of arrows are parallel'

(v) Parallel lines are straight lines that never meet no matter how much they are extended – they are marked with arrowheads to indicate which lines are parallel.

(vi) When a line crosses a pair of parallel lines, there is a relationship between the angles formed – some are equal and others add up to 180°.

All angles *a* are equal.
All angles *b* are equal.
$a + b = 180°$

The terms alternate angles and corresponding angles are used to describe particular pairings of angles:

The two angles marked x are **corresponding angles** – they are in similar positions.

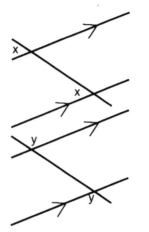

The two angles marked y are **alternate angles** – they are on opposite sides of the cutting line.

2 A **locus** is the path followed (or traced out) by a point as it moves according to some rule. More than one of these paths are called loci. Here are some examples:

  (i) The locus of a point such that it is always the same distance from a line. If there is such a locus on each side of the line, this gives a pair of lines parallel to the original line.

  (ii) The locus of a point such that it is always the same distance from some fixed point. This gives a circle.

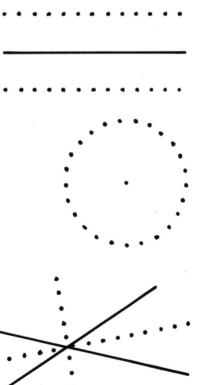

  (iii) The locus of a point such that it is equidistant from a pair of lines. This gives the bisectors of the angles between the lines.

'The important thing is the rule that determines how the line moves – sketch a diagram if it helps you understand the rule'

(iv) The locus of a point such that it is equidistant from two points. This is the perpendicular bisector of the straight line joining the two points.

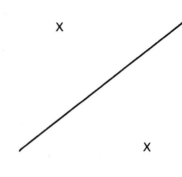

How to Do It

1 In each of the following diagrams find the unknown angle (or angles), and state whether it is an acute angle, an obtuse angle, a reflex angle or a right angle. *Note:* Do not try to measure the angles in the diagrams. They are not necessarily accurate.

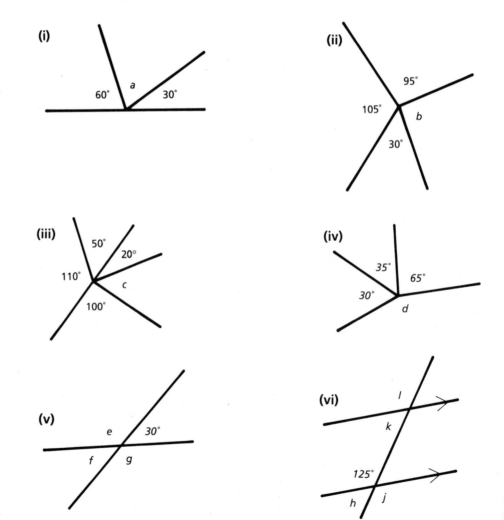

Solution

The angles on a straight line total 180°, so

$$60° + a + 30° = 180°$$
$$a = 90° \quad \text{(a right angle)}$$

(i)

The angles round a point total 360°, so **(ii)**

$$105° + 95° + b + 30° = 360°$$
$$b = 130° \quad \text{(an obtuse angle)}$$

The angles round a point total 360°, so **(iii)**

$$100° + 110° + 50° + 20° + c = 360°$$
$$c = 80° \quad \text{(an acute angle)}$$

The angles round a point total 360°, so

$$30° + 35° + 65° + d = 360°$$
$$d = 230° \quad \text{(a reflex angle)}$$

(iv)

$$e + 30° = 180° \quad \text{(on a straight line)}$$
$$e = 150° \quad \text{(an obtuse angle)}$$
$$f = 30° \quad \text{(opposite angles)}$$
$$\text{(an acute angle)}$$
$$g = 150° \quad \text{(opposite } e)$$
$$\text{(an obtuse angle)}$$

(v)

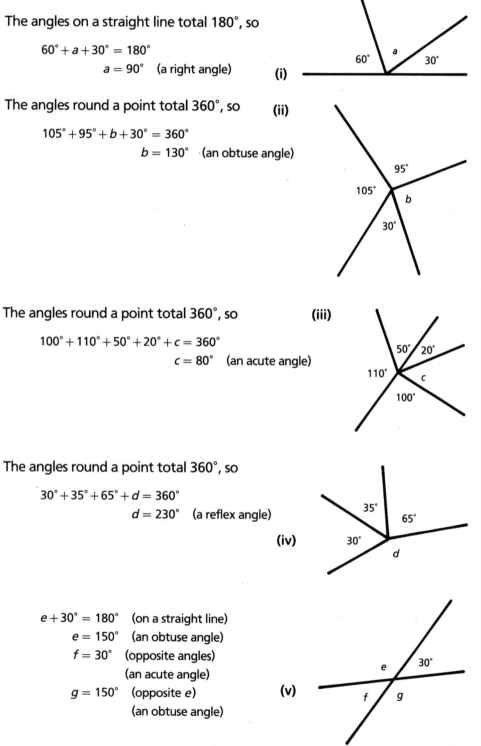

97

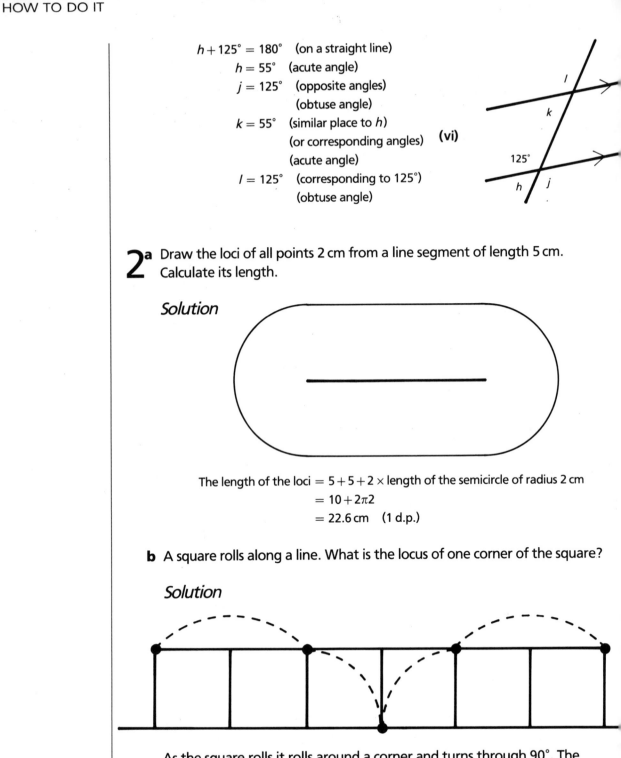

$$h + 125° = 180° \quad \text{(on a straight line)}$$
$$h = 55° \quad \text{(acute angle)}$$
$$j = 125° \quad \text{(opposite angles)}$$
$$\text{(obtuse angle)}$$
$$k = 55° \quad \text{(similar place to } h\text{)}$$
$$\text{(or corresponding angles)} \quad \textbf{(vi)}$$
$$\text{(acute angle)}$$
$$l = 125° \quad \text{(corresponding to 125°)}$$
$$\text{(obtuse angle)}$$

2 **a** Draw the loci of all points 2 cm from a line segment of length 5 cm. Calculate its length.

Solution

The length of the loci $= 5 + 5 + 2 \times$ length of the semicircle of radius 2 cm
$$= 10 + 2\pi 2$$
$$= 22.6 \, \text{cm} \quad \text{(1 d.p.)}$$

b A square rolls along a line. What is the locus of one corner of the square?

Solution

As the square rolls it rolls around a corner and turns through 90°. The corner then follows a quarter-circle each time, sometimes of radius the diagonal of the square and sometimes of radius the side of the square.

c A goat is tethered on a lawn to a point X by a thin chain which is 7 m long. There is a high wall 5 m long as shown in the diagram. Make a scale drawing of the situation and shade in the area of the grass the goat can eat.

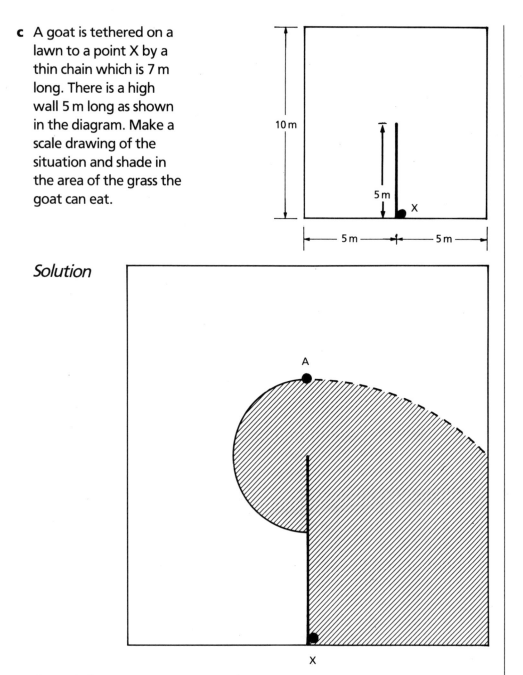

Solution

The scale is 1 cm represents 1 m – from X the goat can go out until the chain is taut; it can then follow an arc until it reaches A. At A the chain is alongside the wall and any further movement left is restricted by the wall, so the goat can now follow a circle whose centre is the end of the wall and radius 2 m. The shaded area represents all the points which the goat can reach.

Do It Yourself

1 Find the angles marked in the following diagrams:

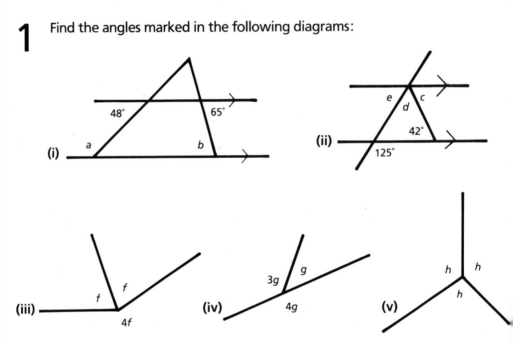

2 **a** A ship is sailing due west at 10 miles/hour. An enemy gun site with a range of 3 miles is 5 miles west and 2 miles north of the ship. Draw a scale drawing, using 1 cm to represent 1 mile, to show the ship's course and the region in which it is in range of the gun. For how long is the ship in danger?

b A ladder of length 20 ft is placed on horizontal ground against a vertical wall. The bottom of the ladder slips away from the wall. Draw a scale diagram of the situation putting in the ladder in five positions. Sketch the locus of the mid-point of the ladder as it slips down.

c A horse is tethered to a round post by a piece of rope. The rope is 10 ft long and the horse walks round the post and as far from it as possible. Draw a sketch to show the path followed by the horse. If the distance round the post is 2 ft how many times can the horse walk round the post?

Triangles, Quadrilaterals and Polygons

Things You Need to Know

1 There are many types of triangle:

  (i) A **scalene** triangle has no sides the same length, and no equal angles.

  (ii) An **acute-angled** triangle has all its angles less than 90°.

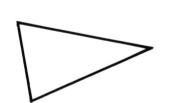

  (iii) A **right-angled** triangle has one angle equal to 90°.

(iv) An **obtuse-angled** triangle has an angle greater than 90°.

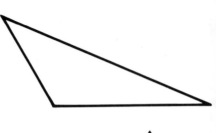

'The longest side of any triangle is opposite the largest angle, and the shortest side is opposite the smallest angle'

(v) An **equilateral** triangle has all sides the same length and all its angles are 60°.

(vi) An **isosceles** triangle has one pair of equal sides and the angles opposite the equal sides are equal to each other.

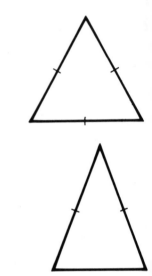

In any triangle the angles total 180°.

2 When constructing a triangle it is a good idea to draw a sketch of the required triangle, putting in the measurements/labels that you have been given. You can draw a triangle given:
  (i) the three sides;
  (ii) two sides and the included angle;
  (iii) a side and any two angles (you would work with the angles at the ends of the given side).

3 A **quadrilateral** is a four-sided shape. There are many different types:
  (i) A **trapezium** has two sides parallel to each other.

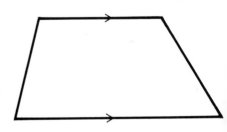

(ii) A **parallelogram** has opposite sides parallel and equal in length, and opposing angles are equal.

(iii) A **rectangle** has all angles equal to 90°, and opposite sides parallel and equal in length (you can think of it as a special parallelogram, where the angles are all 90°).

(iv) A **square** is a rectangle with all sides the same length.

(v) A **rhombus** is a parallelogram with all sides the same length (the diagonals cross at 90°). Some people think of it as a square 'pushed over'.

(vi) A **kite** has two pairs of adjacent sides equal.

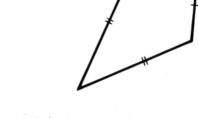

In any quadrilateral the sum of the angles is 360°. (This can be shown by drawing one diagonal, thereby making two triangles. The angles of each triangle total 180° – so for two triangles the total is 360°.)

4 The general name for any shape is a **polygon**. Polygons are named by the number of sides:

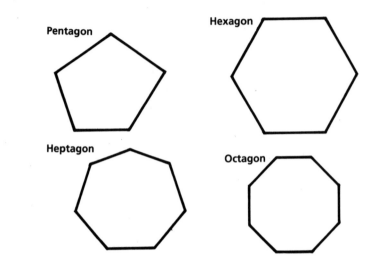

If a polygon is described as regular it means that all sides are the same length and the angles are equal to each other.

The sum of the angles of a polygon with n sides is given by the formula

$$180°n - 360°$$

The sum of the exterior angles of any polygon is 360°.

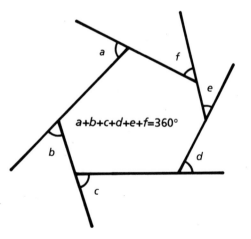

$$a+b+c+d+e+f=360°$$

Some types of regular polygon will fit together, like tiles, to form a regular pattern with no gaps between them. This is known as a **tessellation**. Every triangle and quadrilateral will tessellate, and so will regular hexagons.

5 The most important shape of all is probably the right-angled triangle. Pythagoras' theorem gives a rule connecting the three sides of a right-angled triangle.

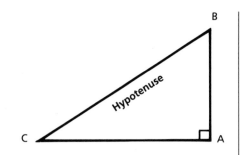

Calling side BC *a* (it is opposite angle A) then side AC will be *b* and side AB will be *c*. Then

$$a^2 = b^2 + c^2$$

The best known right-angled triangles have sides:

3 units, 4 units and hypotenuse 5 units
5 units, 12 units and hypotenuse 13 units

6 Right-angled triangles also have rules connecting the angles and the sides. Remember that the side opposite the right angle is the hypotenuse. If we call the side next to the given angle the adjacent side, and the other side the opposite side, then we can find three relationships between sides and angles in right-angled triangles. These are the **trigonometric ratios**: **sine** (sin), **cosine** (cos) and **tangent** (tan) of an angle.

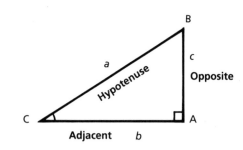

$$\sin = \frac{\text{Opposite}}{\text{Hypotenuse}} = \frac{O}{H}$$

$$\cos = \frac{\text{Adjacent}}{\text{Hypotenuse}} = \frac{A}{H}$$

$$\tan = \frac{\text{Opposite}}{\text{Adjacent}} = \frac{O}{A}$$

$$\sin C = \frac{c}{a} \qquad \cos C = \frac{b}{a} \qquad \tan C = \frac{c}{b}$$

The equations can be rearranged, to give the following:

$$\text{opposite} = \text{hypotenuse} \times \sin$$
$$\text{adjacent} = \text{hypotenuse} \times \cos$$
$$\text{opposite} = \text{adjacent} \times \tan$$

You must ensure that you can use a calculator to find the sin (or cos or tan) of an angle; and also, if given the sin (or cos or tan) of an angle, find the angle (use inv sin, etc.). When using a calculator, it is good practice to use full accuracy throughout the calculation and, at the final stages to give the answer to three significant figures unless told otherwise.

How to Do It

1 Find the angle x in each of the following triangles, and also say what sort of triangle it is.

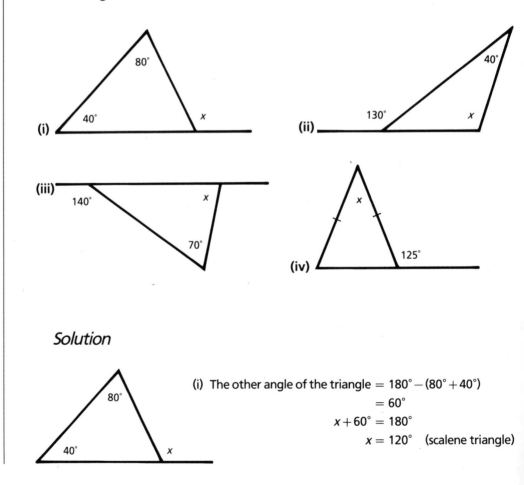

Solution

(i) The other angle of the triangle $= 180° - (80° + 40°)$
$$= 60°$$
$$x + 60° = 180°$$
$$x = 120° \quad \text{(scalene triangle)}$$

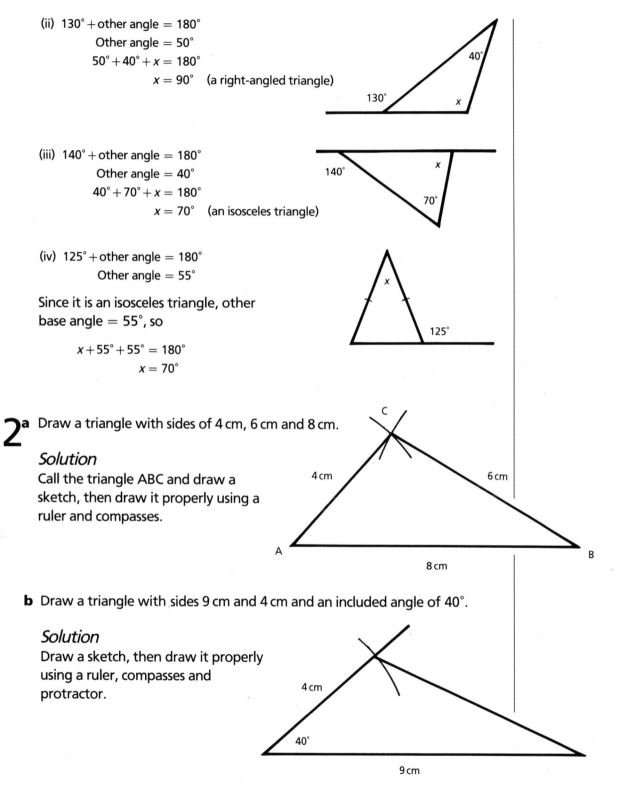

(ii) $130° +$ other angle $= 180°$
       Other angle $= 50°$
       $50° + 40° + x = 180°$
                $x = 90°$ (a right-angled triangle)

(iii) $140° +$ other angle $= 180°$
       Other angle $= 40°$
       $40° + 70° + x = 180°$
                $x = 70°$ (an isosceles triangle)

(iv) $125° +$ other angle $= 180°$
       Other angle $= 55°$

Since it is an isosceles triangle, other
base angle $= 55°$, so

       $x + 55° + 55° = 180°$
                    $x = 70°$

2 **a** Draw a triangle with sides of 4 cm, 6 cm and 8 cm.

Solution
Call the triangle ABC and draw a
sketch, then draw it properly using a
ruler and compasses.

b Draw a triangle with sides 9 cm and 4 cm and an included angle of 40°.

Solution
Draw a sketch, then draw it properly
using a ruler, compasses and
protractor.

107

3a In the diagram ABCD is a parallelogram. Calculate the angles x and y.

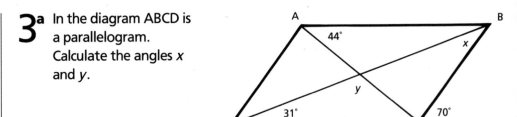

Solution

$$31° + x + \text{angle BCD} = 180°$$
$$\text{angle BCD} = 180° - 70°$$
$$= 110°$$
$$\therefore \quad x = 39°$$

$$\text{angle ACD} = 44° \quad \text{(parallel lines)}$$
$$31° + 44° + y = 180°$$
$$y = 105°$$

b In a quadrilateral one angle is 60° and the other three angles are all equal to each other. What is the size of the other angles?

Solution
Let a be the size of the other angles, so

$$3a + 60° = 360° \quad \text{(angles of a quadrilateral total 360°)}$$
$$3a = 300°$$

so the other angles are each 100°.

4a The interior angle of a regular polygon is 140°. How many sides has the polygon?

Solution
This is easier if we use the exterior angle, which is 40°. The exterior angles of any polygon total 360°, so

$$\text{Number of sides} = \frac{360°}{40°}$$
$$= 9$$

140°

b A polygon has *n* sides, two of the angles are right angles and each of the other angles is 144°. Calculate the number of sides in the polygon.

Solution
Again, it is easier to use the exterior angles. The exterior angles are 90°, 90° and some number of 36° – these must total 360°. So

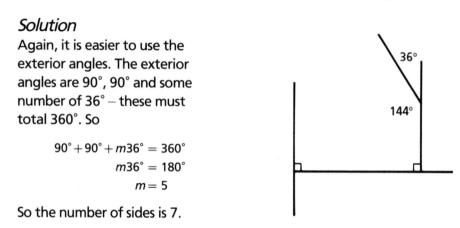

$$90° + 90° + m36° = 360°$$
$$m36° = 180°$$
$$m = 5$$

So the number of sides is 7.

5 For each of the following diagrams find the unknown length marked *d*, correct to three significant figures.

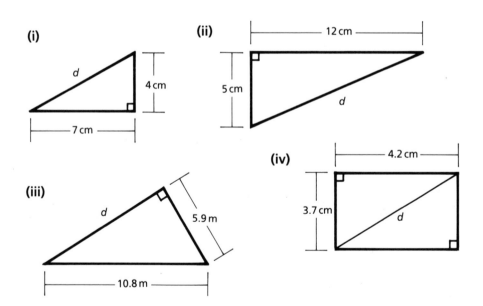

(i)

d

4 cm

7 cm

(ii)

12 cm

5 cm

d

(iii)

d

5.9 m

10.8 m

(iv)

4.2 cm

3.7 cm

d

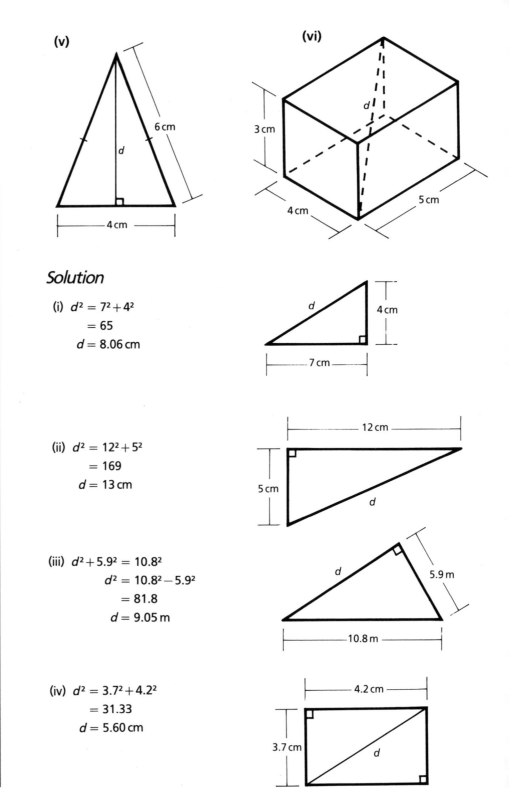

(v)

6 cm

d

4 cm

(vi)

3 cm

d

4 cm

5 cm

Solution

(i) $d^2 = 7^2 + 4^2$
$= 65$
$d = 8.06\,\text{cm}$

d

4 cm

7 cm

(ii) $d^2 = 12^2 + 5^2$
$= 169$
$d = 13\,\text{cm}$

12 cm

5 cm

d

(iii) $d^2 + 5.9^2 = 10.8^2$
$d^2 = 10.8^2 - 5.9^2$
$= 81.8$
$d = 9.05\,\text{m}$

d

5.9 m

10.8 m

(iv) $d^2 = 3.7^2 + 4.2^2$
$= 31.33$
$d = 5.60\,\text{cm}$

4.2 cm

3.7 cm

d

'Make sure you are able to use a calculator to find both squares and square roots'

(v) This is an isosceles triangle in which the height bisects the base, so

$$d^2 + 2^2 = 6^2$$
$$d^2 = 32$$
$$d = 5.66\,\text{cm}$$

(vi) In triangle ABC if AC is called l

$$l^2 = 4^2 + 5^2$$
$$l^2 = 41$$

In triangle ACD

$$d^2 = l^2 + 3^2$$
$$= 41 + 9$$
$$= 50$$
$$d = 7.07\,\text{cm}$$

6 **a** Here is the symmetrical cross-section of an embankment. Calculate the angle x made by the sloping sides with the horizontal.

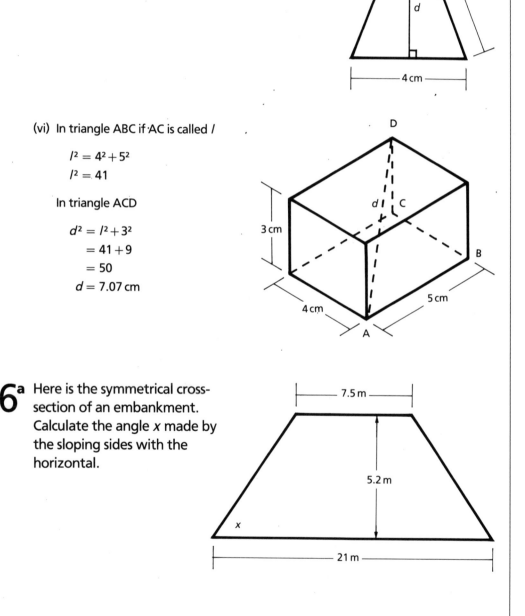

> *'Whenever you are doing any question involving a shape, always draw a reasonable sketch of the shape'*

Solution

We need to make a right-angled triangle – drop a line vertically down from a top corner:

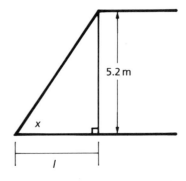

$$l + 7.5 + l = 21$$
$$l = 6.75 \text{ m}$$

So

$$\tan x = \frac{5.2}{6.75}$$

$$x = \tan^{-1}\left(\frac{5.2}{6.75}\right)$$

$$= 37.6°$$

b Using a calculator draw up a table showing the sine of angles from 0° to 360° in steps of 30°. Draw a graph to illustrate the results.

Solution

Angle	0	30	60	90	120	150	180
Sine	0	0.5	0.87	1	0.87	0.5	0

Angle	210	240	270	300	330	360
Sine	−0.5	−0.87	−1	−0.87	−0.5	0

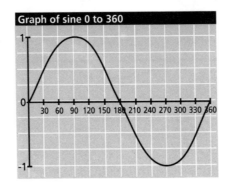

Graph of sine 0 to 360

c A parallelogram JKLM has an area of 36 cm². The sides are of length 8 cm and 5 cm. Calculate:

(i) the perpendicular distance between the longer sides;
(ii) the perpendicular distance between the shorter sides;
(iii) the acute angle between the long and short sides.

Solution

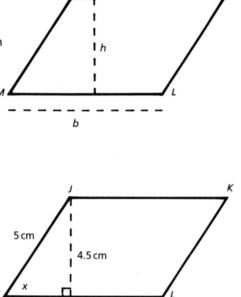

(i)   Area $= b \times h$

If the base is the longer side (8 cm) then

$h = 36 \div 8$
$ = 4.5$ cm

(ii) If the base is the shorter side then

$h = 36 \div 5$
$ = 7.2$ cm

(iii) $\sin x = \dfrac{4.5}{5}$

$ = 0.9$
$x = 64.2°$

Do It Yourself

1 Find the angles marked with letters:

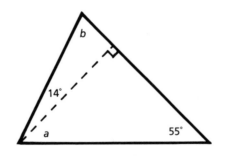

2 Construct a triangle LMN such that LM = 10 cm, MN = 11 cm and LN = 12 cm. Measure the angle LMN.

'When you do a drawing make sure your pencil is sharp, your ruler has a good edge and your compasses don't move too easily'

3 Find the angles marked with letters:

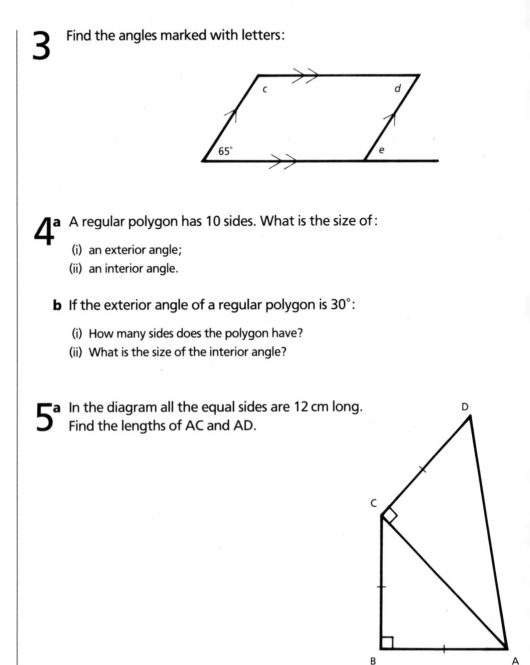

4 **a** A regular polygon has 10 sides. What is the size of:

(i) an exterior angle;

(ii) an interior angle.

b If the exterior angle of a regular polygon is 30°:

(i) How many sides does the polygon have?

(ii) What is the size of the interior angle?

5 **a** In the diagram all the equal sides are 12 cm long. Find the lengths of AC and AD.

b A gift pack of three bottles is shown in the diagram. The larger bottles have a radius of 12 cm and the smaller bottle has a radius of 4 cm. All the bottles are 20 cm high. By joining the centres of the circles representing the bottles, or otherwise, calculate the dimensions of the gift pack. (*Hint:* joining the centres produces what sort of triangle?)

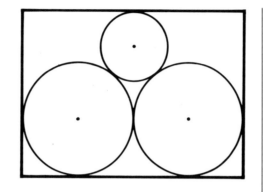

6 **a** Find the angles marked with a letter:

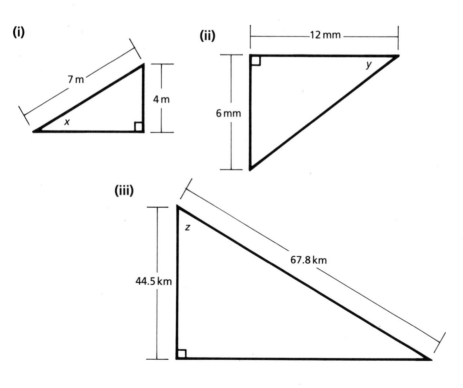

(i)

7 m

4 m

x

(ii)

12 mm

6 mm

y

(iii)

44.5 km

67.8 km

z

b Find the sides marked with a letter:

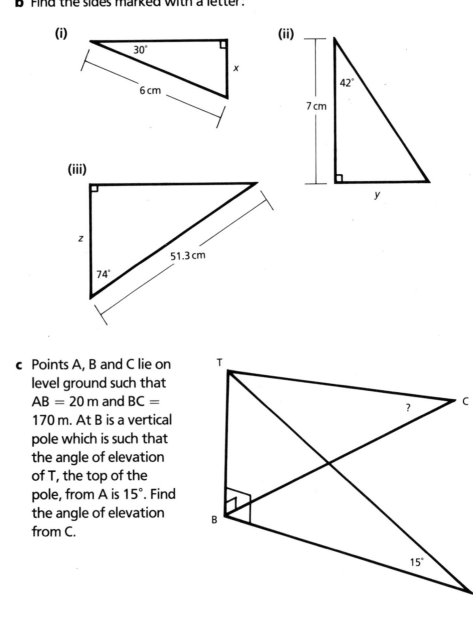

(i)

30°

6 cm

x

(ii)

7 cm

42°

y

(iii)

z

74°

51.3 cm

c Points A, B and C lie on level ground such that AB = 20 m and BC = 170 m. At B is a vertical pole which is such that the angle of elevation of T, the top of the pole, from A is 15°. Find the angle of elevation from C.

T

?

C

B

15°

A

Circles

Things You Need to Know

1 The words you should know are illustrated below:

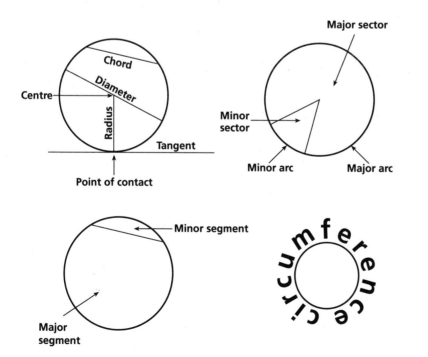

2 In doing calculations the value of π is often used. This will either be given to you (3.14, or something close to this) or you should use the value given by your calculator. You will be provided with formulae for use in the examinations, but you do need to be familiar with them.

Using r for the length of the radius:

Diameter $= 2r$
Circumference $= \pi d$　or　$2\pi r$
Area of circle $= \pi r^2$

(π is a number that continues for ever. We normally use 3.14: your calculator will give you a much more accurate figure.)

'The angle between a tangent and radius is 90°'

3 There are lots of properties of angles that are based around the circle. Here are the ones you should be able to use:

  (i) A tangent is perpendicular to the radius at the point of contact.

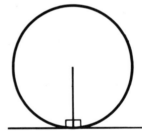

  (ii) The angle formed from a diameter to the circumference is always a right angle.

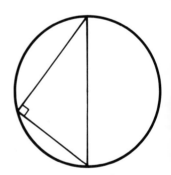

(iii) The angle given at the centre by an arc or chord is twice the angle given at the circumference.

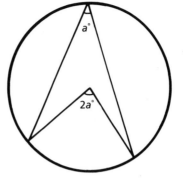

(iv) Opposite angles of a quadrilateral in a circle total 180°. This type of quadrilateral is called a cyclic quadrilateral.

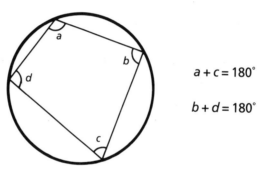

$$a + c = 180°$$

$$b + d = 180°$$

(v) A line from the centre of the circle to the mid-point of a chord is perpendicular to the chord.

(vi) Equal-length chords are the same distance from the centre of the circle.

119

(vii) The two tangents from an external point are the same length and the angles marked are equal.

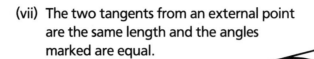

How to Do It

1 On the diagrams various parts of the circle are labelled *a*, *b*, *c* and *d*. What are the correct labels for *a*, *b*, *c* and *d*?

Solution

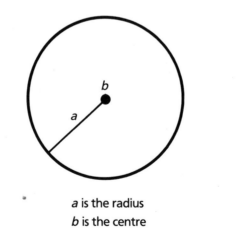

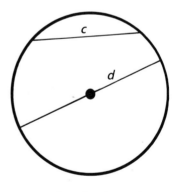

a is the radius
b is the centre

c is a chord
d is the diameter

2a A circular running track has a radius of 40 m. What is the distance round the track? What area of grass is inside the track?

Solution

Distance round track = circumference of circle
$$= 2 \times \pi \times 40$$
$$= 251 \, \text{m} \quad (3 \, \text{s.f.})$$

Area inside track $= \pi \times 40^2$
$$= 5030 \, \text{m}^2 \quad (3 \, \text{s.f.})$$

b A tray of length 45 cm and width 55 cm has rounded corners of radius 2.5 cm. What is the perimeter of the tray and what area does it cover?

Solution

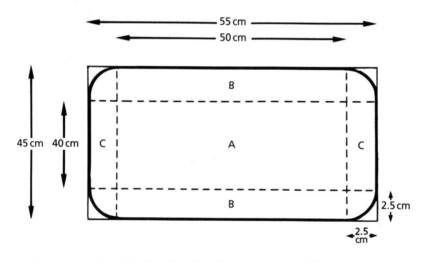

Perimeter $= 2 \times 40 + 2 \times 50 + 4 \times \text{distance round } \frac{1}{4} \text{ circles}$
$$= 180 + 2 \times \pi \times 2.5$$
$$= 196 \, \text{cm} \quad (3 \, \text{s.f.})$$

Area $= A + 2B + 2C + \text{area of 4 quarter-circles}$
$$= 40 \times 50 + 2 \times (50 \times 2.5) + 2 \times (40 \times 2.5) + \pi \times 2.5^2$$
$$= 2470 \, \text{cm}^2$$

3 **a** Find the lettered angles in the following diagrams – O denotes the centre of the circle.

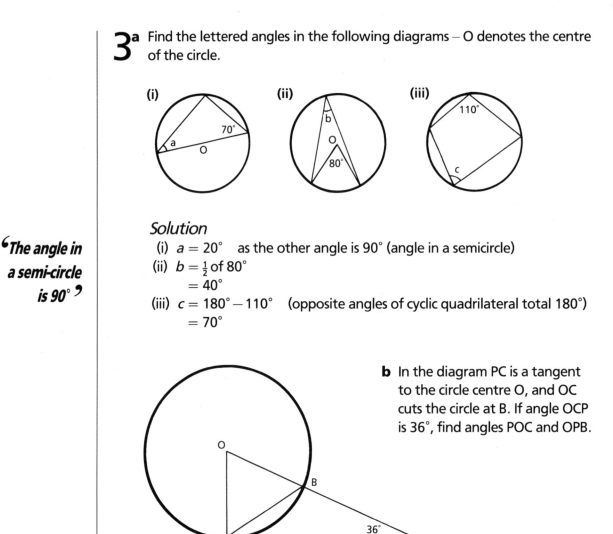

(i)   (ii)   (iii)

The angle in a semi-circle is 90°

Solution

(i) $a = 20°$ as the other angle is 90° (angle in a semicircle)

(ii) $b = \frac{1}{2}$ of 80°

$\quad = 40°$

(iii) $c = 180° - 110°$ (opposite angles of cyclic quadrilateral total 180°)

$\quad = 70°$

b In the diagram PC is a tangent to the circle centre O, and OC cuts the circle at B. If angle OCP is 36°, find angles POC and OPB.

Solution

OP is a radius, PC is a tangent, hence they are at right angles.

$$\text{Angle POC} = 180° - 90° - 36°$$
$$= 54°$$

OP and OB are both radii – hence equal in length, thus making OPB an isosceles triangle. So angles OPB and OBP are equal:

$$\text{Angle OPB} = \frac{1}{2}(180° - 54°)$$
$$= 63°$$

c Find the marked angle in the
following diagram:

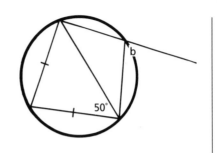

Solution

Firstly label some of the other angles:

$$y = 50° \quad \text{(angle in isosceles triangle)}$$

so
$$x + 50° + 50° = 180°$$
$$x = 80°$$
$$x + z = 180° \quad \text{(opposite angles of cyclic quadrilateral)}$$
$$z = 100°$$

so
$$b = 80° \quad \text{(angles on straight line)}$$

Do It Yourself

1 The following words are anagrams of some special words for the circle. The
first is done for you as an example:

   (i) RECENT   Centre
   (ii) DARUSI
   (iii) TENGNAT
   (iv) NORMI CAR
   (v) AIDMERET
   (vi) STRECO

2a The hour hand of a clock is 2.75 cm long. How far does it travel in 6 hours?

   b If the total distance round a circular bowl is 28 cm, find the radius of the
   bowl.

c A circular race track has an inner radius of 45 m and an outer radius of 50 m. What is the difference in length in running one lap on the outer edge compared to one lap on the inner edge?

d A piece of metal 125 mm square has a circle of diameter 75 mm cut out of it. What is the area of metal left?

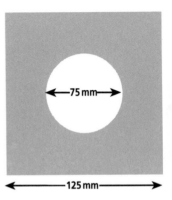

←—75 mm—→

←——————125 mm——————→

e A piece of metal has the cross-section shown in the diagram. Calculate the area of the cross-section.

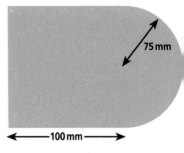

75 mm

←——100 mm——→

3 a The diagram shows a quadrilateral drawn round a circle. Show that AB + CD = BC + AD.

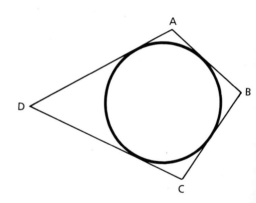

b A circle is drawn inside a triangle so that the sides of the triangle are tangents of the circle. If the triangle formed by the points of contact has angles of 55°, 63° and 62°, find the angles of the original triangle.

(Hint: draw a line from each point of contact of the tangent to the centre of the circle. Can you find the angles at the centre?)

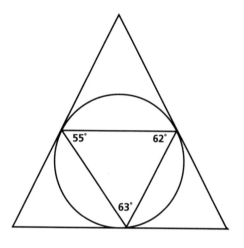

14 Transformation and Symmetry

Things You Need to Know

1 A shape, or object, has **line symmetry** if it is possible to place a straight line such that one side is a reflection of the other. Sometimes a shape may have more than one line (or 'axis') of symmetry:

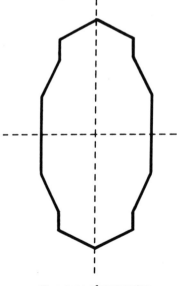

Two axes of symmetry

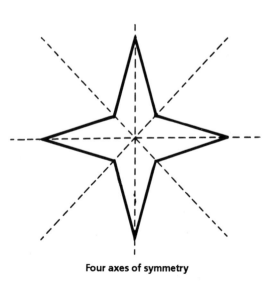

Four axes of symmetry

2 A **translation** simply moves the position of the object, without any turning or twisting, the object simply 'sliding' to the new position on the grid. It can be described in words ('move it along 4 to the right and 2 upwards') or it can be given as a vector movement, as shown:

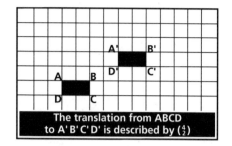

The translation from ABCD to A'B'C'D' is described by $\binom{4}{2}$

The translated shape is identical to the original in all respects.

3 A shape, or object, is reflected in a **mirror line**. Straight lines joining corresponding points will cross the mirror line at right angles and be bisected by it.

The size of the reflected object is the same as the original, but the direction of the shape is opposite, i.e. left and right have been switched over, just like in a mirror.

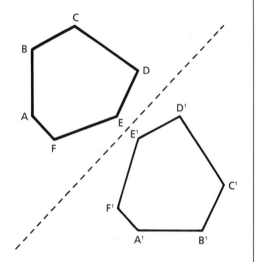

4 An object has **rotational symmetry** if it can be turned around some point so that it fits back to the original shape with a turn of less than 360°.

The order of rotational symmetry is the number of times this can be done as the object is rotated through 360°.

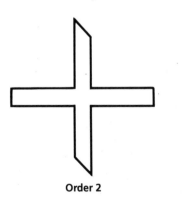

Order 2

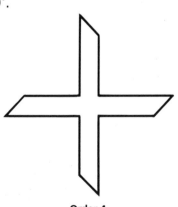

Order 4

Order 3

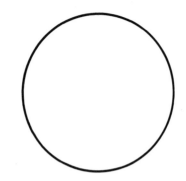

Order? Well, its a very large number: infinity!

'Congruent shapes are identical'

5 A shape that is identical to another is known as a **congruent shape**. This means that corresponding sides of the shape have the same length *and* corresponding angles are equal.

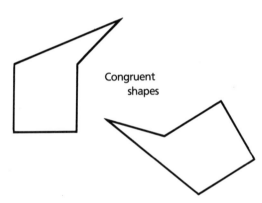

Congruent shapes

6 When the size of an object is changed but the shape stays the same this is termed an **enlargement**. An enlargement must have a centre of enlargement and an enlargement factor. If the enlargement factor is greater than 1 then the image produced will be larger than the original object; however, if the enlargement factor is between 0 and 1 then the image produced will be smaller than the original.

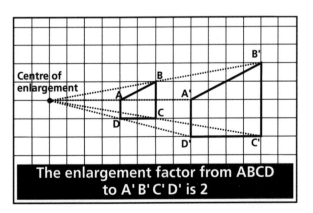

Centre of enlargement

The enlargement factor from ABCD to A'B'C'D' is 2

When a shape or object has been enlarged it produces a shape which is identical to the original with the exception that it is larger – it is known as a **similar shape**. A similar shape has corresponding angles equal and the lengths of corresponding sides are all in the *same* ratio – this ratio is called the **scale factor**. The scale factor can be found by means of the following formula:

$$\text{Scale factor} = \frac{\text{length of side on enlargement}}{\text{length of side on original}}$$

'A scale factor can also be less than 1 to give a smaller shape'

How to Do It

1 a Complete the following shapes, where the dotted line (or lines) represents a line (or lines) of symmetry:

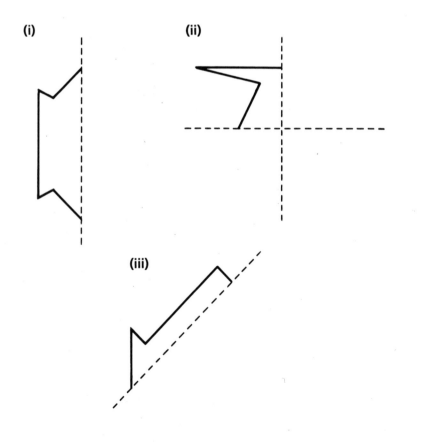

(i)

(ii)

(iii)

> *'A shape is symmetrical about a line when one half of it is a reflection of the other half'*

Solution

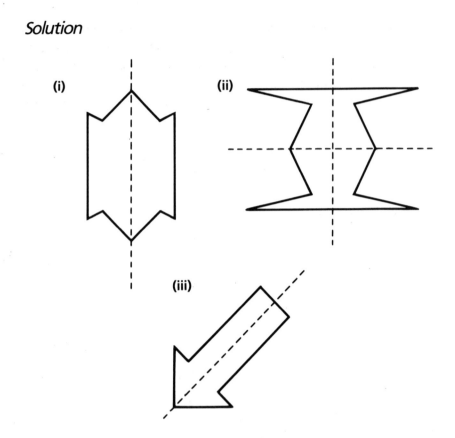

(i)

(ii)

(iii)

b The diagram shows a square, a rhombus, an isosceles trapezium (sloping sides the same length), an equilateral triangle, an isosceles triangle and a regular hexagon. Make a copy of each shape and on it draw all the axes of symmetry.

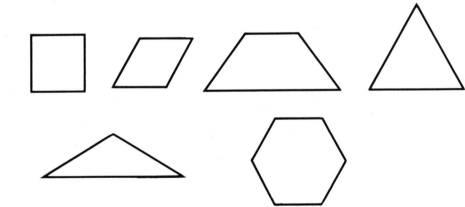

Solution

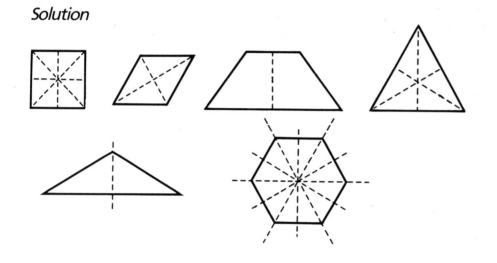

2 The diagram shows a
4 × 6 lettered grid.
 (i) What translation
takes G to L?
 (ii) What translation
takes T to K?
 (iii) A translation takes
S to P. Where does
this same
translation take G?
What was taken to
R by this
translation?

A	B	C	D	E	F
G	H	I	J	K	L
M	N	O	P	Q	R
S	T	U	V	W	X

Solution

 (i) 5 to the right
 (ii) 3 right and 2 up
 (iii) The translation is 3 to the right and 1 up so G goes to D and it was U that was
taken to R.

3 Show the reflection of the shape in the mirror line M₁M₂. The point P is marked on the shape; mark its reflected position with P′.

Solution

4 Which of the following shapes has rotational symmetry? Make a sketch of those that do and give the order of the symmetry.

'The order of symmetry is the number of times a shape fits back to its original shape when rotated through 360°'

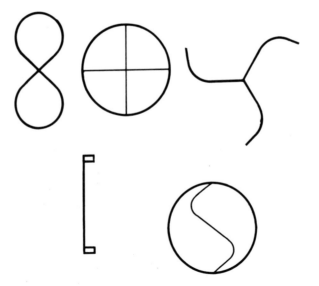

Solution

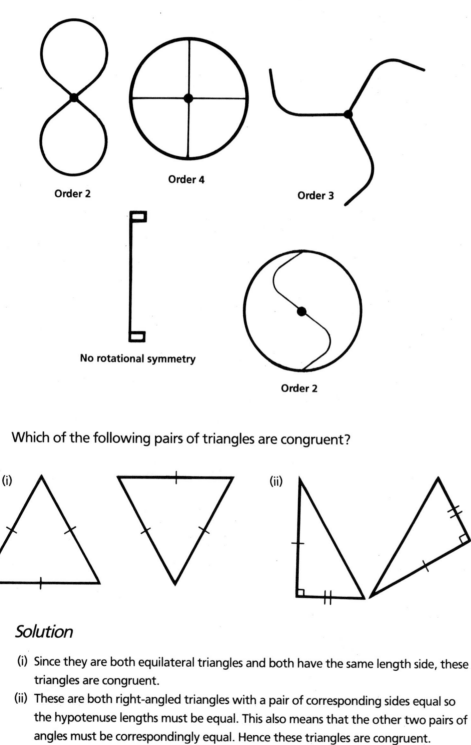

Order 2

Order 4

Order 3

No rotational symmetry

Order 2

5 Which of the following pairs of triangles are congruent?

(i)

(ii)

Solution

(i) Since they are both equilateral triangles and both have the same length side, these triangles are congruent.

(ii) These are both right-angled triangles with a pair of corresponding sides equal so the hypotenuse lengths must be equal. This also means that the other two pairs of angles must be correspondingly equal. Hence these triangles are congruent.

6 **a** The letter F is shown on the grid. Enlarge it by a factor of 2 using the point P as the centre of enlargement.

Take two corresponding pairs of measurements and show that the scale factor is 2.

Solution

The length of the top bar of the F is 3 units in the original and 6 units in the enlarged:

$$6 \div 3 = 2$$

The height of the F is 4 units in the original and 8 units in the enlarged:

$$6 \div 3 = 2$$

b A tree casts a shadow that is 15 m long. At the same time a metre rule held upright and touching the ground casts a shadow 75 cm long. What is the height of the tree?

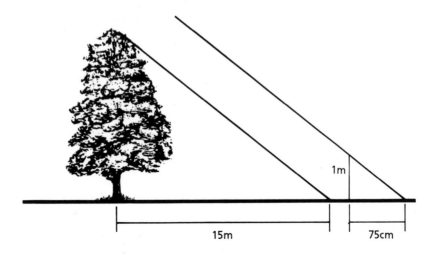

15m   1m   75cm

Solution

The two triangles formed by the tree/ground/sun ray and the stick/ground/sun ray are similar.

$$\text{Scale factor} = \frac{\text{length of side on enlargement}}{\text{length of side on original}}$$
$$= \frac{15}{0.75}$$
$$= 20$$

So everything in the 'tree triangle' is 20 times larger than the equivalent length in the 'stick triangle'. As the stick corresponds to the tree and the stick is 1 m long therefore the tree is 20 m high.

Do It Yourself

1 Using six squares, and arranging them so that they touch along their sides, how many shapes can you produce that have line symmetry? How many of your shapes have two lines of symmetry? Here is one done for you:

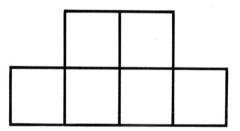

2 On a sheet of graph paper draw and mark axes from -5 to 10. On the paper draw the triangle with vertices A(1, 1), B(3, 2) and C(1, 5). Draw the triangles obtained by applying the following translations:

(i) 3 upwards;
(ii) 4 to the left;
(iii) 2 downwards and 4 to the right.

3 a Draw the image of each of the given shapes when reflected in the dotted line.

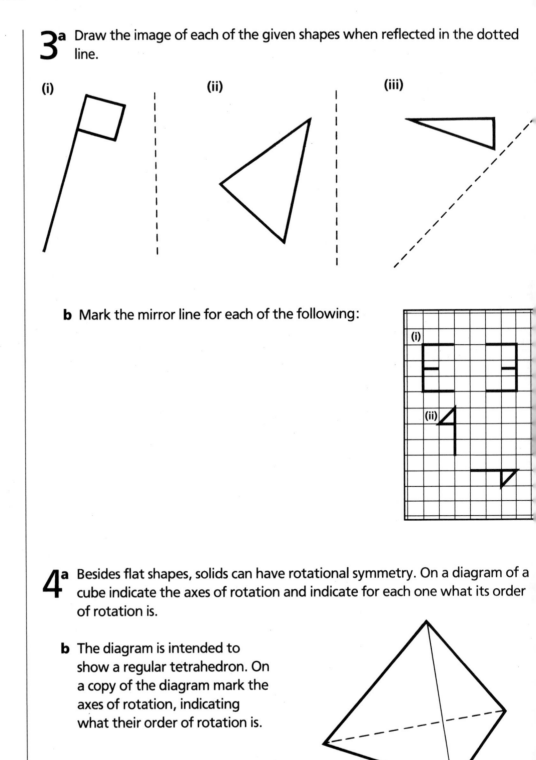

(i)

(ii)

(iii)

b Mark the mirror line for each of the following:

(i)

(ii)

4 a Besides flat shapes, solids can have rotational symmetry. On a diagram of a cube indicate the axes of rotation and indicate for each one what its order of rotation is.

b The diagram is intended to show a regular tetrahedron. On a copy of the diagram mark the axes of rotation, indicating what their order of rotation is.

5 A cuboid consists of six rectangles. Draw an outline of a cuboid and indicate which faces are congruent to each other.

6a Enlarge each of the following shapes by the factor given using C as the centre of enlargement.

'The scale factor is a multiple of the lengths'

(i)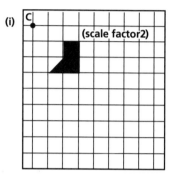
(scale factor 2)

(ii)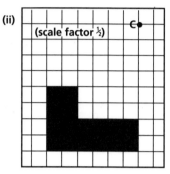
(scale factor ½)

b In the diagram the triangles ABC and EFG are similar. If the area of triangle ABC is 8 cm² calculate the area of triangle EFG.

   (*Hint:* the area of a triangle is given by halving the base and multiplying by the height. Find the base of ABC and use the scale factor – which you have to find – to calculate the base of EFG. Now work out its area.)

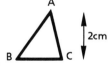

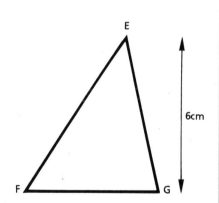

15 Areas and Volumes

Things You Need to Know

1 You should be able to recognise the following shapes:

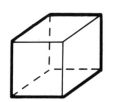

Cube

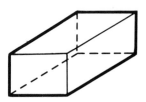

Cuboid

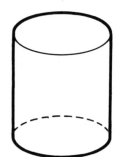

Cylinder

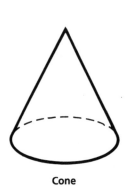

Cone

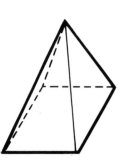

Square pyramid

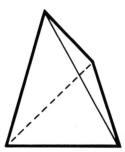

Triangular Pyramid
(or tetrahedron)

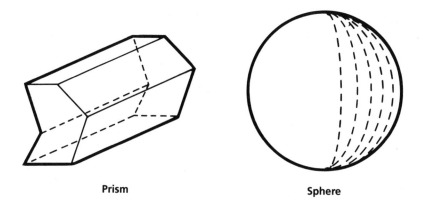

Prism

Sphere

2 We measure the **area** of a surface in **square centimetres** (cm²). For the basic shapes there are standard formulae that are used:

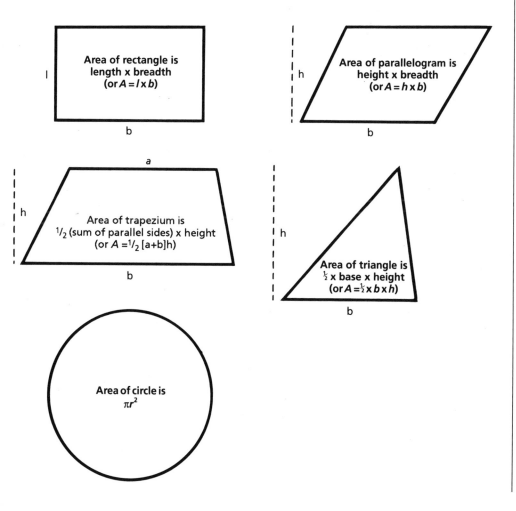

l

b

Area of rectangle is
length x breadth
(or $A = l \times b$)

h

b

Area of parallelogram is
height x breadth
(or $A = h \times b$)

a

h

b

Area of trapezium is
$^1/_2$ (sum of parallel sides) x height
(or $A = {}^1/_2 [a+b]h$)

h

b

Area of triangle is
½ x base x height
(or $A = \frac{1}{2} \times b \times h$)

Area of circle is
πr^2

3 The **volume** of a three-dimensional shape is measured in **cubic centimetres** (cm³). For the basic objects there are standard formulae for the volume:

$V = lbh$

$V =$ area of cross–section x length

$V = \pi r^2 h$

$V = \frac{1}{3}$ base area x height

$V = \frac{4}{3}\pi r^3$

You do not need to remember any of these formulae as they will be given to you in the examination – but you do need to be familiar with them.

How to Do It

1 Surfaces can be either flat or curved. For each of the following shapes say how many flat surfaces and how many curved surfaces it has.

  (i) a cube (ii) a cylinder (iii) a square pyramid (iv) a cone

Solution

 (i) A cube has six flat surfaces and no curved surfaces.

 (ii) A cylinder has two flat surfaces and one curved surface.

 (iii) A square pyramid has five flat surfaces and no curved surfaces.

 (iv) A cone has one flat surface and one curved surface.

2a A photograph, 20 cm by 14 cm, is placed in a frame which is 22 cm by 16 cm. What is the area of the border?

Solution

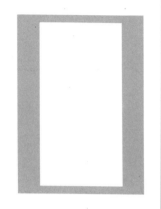

$$\text{Area of frame} = 16 \times 22 \text{ cm}^2$$
$$= 352 \text{ cm}^2$$
$$\text{Area of photo} = 20 \times 14 \text{ cm}^2$$
$$= 280 \text{ cm}^2$$
$$\text{Area of border} = 352 - 280 \text{ cm}^2$$
$$= 72 \text{ cm}^2$$

b A circular picture of radius 7 cm is put into the frame in question 2a. What is the area of the border now?

Solution

$$\text{Area of frame} = 352 \text{ cm}^2$$
$$\text{Area of picture} = \pi \times 7^2 \text{ cm}^2$$
$$= 154 \text{ cm}^2 \quad (3 \text{ s.f.})$$
$$\text{Area of border} = 352 - 154 \text{ cm}^2$$
$$= 198 \text{ cm}^2$$

c The parallelogram ABCD has its vertices at (1, 1), (2, 3), (5, 3) and (4, 1). Find its area.

Solution

Area of parallelogram = base × perpendicular height, so with base = 3 units and height = 2 units,

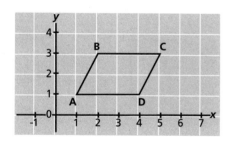

$$\text{Area} = 6 \text{ units}^2$$

141

3 a The surface of a pond is a square of side 150 cm. During a very cold spell the pond froze to a depth of 2.5 cm. Find the mass of the ice, given that the density of ice is 0.9 g/cm³.

Solution

$$\text{Volume of ice} = 150 \times 150 \times 2.5 \text{ cm}^3$$
$$= 56\,250 \text{ cm}^3$$
$$\text{Mass of the ice} = 0.9 \times 56\,250 \text{ g}$$
$$= 50\,625 \text{ g}$$
$$= 50.625 \text{ kg}$$

b An ingot of steel whose volume is 2 m³ is rolled to a plate 15 mm thick and 1.75 m wide. Find the length of the steel in metres.

Solution

$$\text{Volume of ingot} = 2 \text{ m}^3$$
$$\text{so volume of plate} = 2 \text{ m}^3$$

Changing the measurements of the plate so that they are in metres,

$$2 = 1.75 \times 0.015 \times \text{length of plate}$$
$$\text{Length of plate} = \frac{2}{0.02625}$$
$$= 76.2 \text{ m} \quad (3 \text{ s.f.})$$

Do It Yourself

1 A **net** is a flat shape that can be folded to form a three-dimensional solid. For each of the following shapes draw a net, cut it out and fold to see if it works.

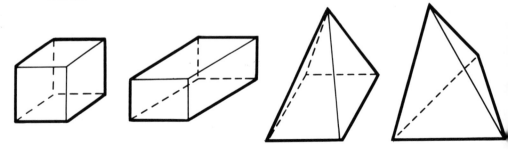

2 a A triangle has sides of 3 cm, 4 cm and 5 cm. Show that it is a right-angled triangle and hence calculate its area.

b The diagram shows a 4 cm square with a diagonal band which is 1.5 cm from the corners.

Find:

(i) the perimeter of the square;
(ii) the unshaded area;
(iii) the area of the shaded band;
(iv) the width of the band.

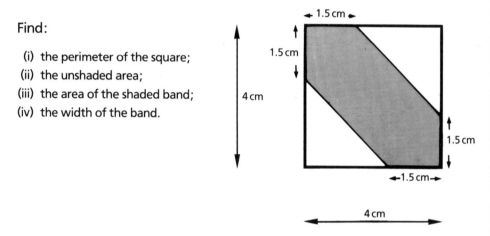

c A metal disc with radius 5 cm comes to rest with its centre 3 cm from the edge of the table. Calculate the area of the disc on the table.

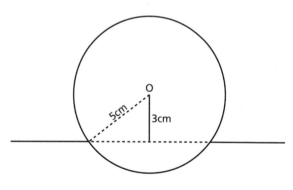

'A complex shape can often be broken up into simple ones – so add the areas of the simple shapes to give the complex one. Don't forget to subtract for any holes'

3 a What is the surface area of a solid cube whose volume is 64 cm³?

b A concrete gully is to be made in the shape indicated in the diagram.

Calculate:

(i) the cross-sectional area;
(ii) the volume of the gully;
(iii) the mass of the gully if 1 cm³ of concrete has a mass of 6 g.

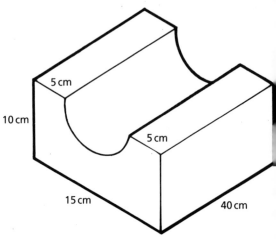

10 cm

5 cm

5 cm

15 cm

40 cm

c A container consists of a cylinder of radius 10 cm and height 15 cm, with a conical top of height 25 cm. What is its volume?

Algebra

Things You Need to Know

1 Algebra is a type of mathematical shorthand using letters to represent numbers.

Only like terms can be added/subtracted. For example:

$$2x + 5x = 7x$$
$$9xy - 4xy = 5xy$$

But $10a^2b + 7ab^2$ is just that, we *cannot* add the terms.

The multiplication sign ($\times$) can easily be mistaken for the letter x so we normally would not write in the multiplication sign. This means that if there are two things without a sign between them then they are being multiplied. Thus,

$$8a^3b^2 \times 2a^2b = 8a^3b^22a^2b = 16a^5b^3$$

Dividing is simply a matter of putting it down as a fraction and cancelling:

$$\frac{8a^3b^2}{2a^2b^3} = \frac{4a}{b}$$

2 **Brackets** are used to indicate that the contents should be treated like a single term. For example, 'think of a number, double it and add 7, then treble the result,' could be written as follows, using x for the number you thought of:

$3(2x+7)$

Sometimes the brackets need to be removed. This is done by *each term inside the brackets being multiplied by the term outside*. Here is a visual way of showing how it works:

$3(2x+7) = 6x+7$

Sometimes we need to multiply together two brackets, like this:

$(2x+y)(3x-2y)$

We can rewrite it as

$2x(3x-2y)+y(3x-2y)$

and this becomes

$6x^2-4xy+3xy-2y^2$

By collecting like terms, this simplifies to

$6x^2-xy-2y^2$

In other words, the rule is the same but the term outside the brackets is the contents of the other pair of brackets. The way it works can be shown visually as follows:

$$(2x+y)(3x-2y) = 6x^2-4xy+3xy-2y^2$$
$$= 6x^2-xy-2y^2$$

The process of multiplying out brackets is known as **expanding** them.

> **'You must do the same to both sides of the equation'**

3 The aim with equations is to rearrange them so that the terms involving the letter are on one side and the numbers are on the other. *Remember that you must do the same thing to each side of the equation.*

Here is another example:

$$\frac{3(5t-4)}{t+8} = 3$$ (Don't remove the brackets – it is better to deal with the division. Multiply both sides by $(t+8)$.)

$3(5t-4) = 3(t+8)$ (now we can expand the brackets)

$15t-12 = 3t+24$ (rearrange, letter terms on one side)

$15t-3t-12 = 24$ (rearrange, numbers on the other side)

$15t-3t = 24+12$ (tidy up each side)

$12t = 36$ (divide both sides by 12)

$t = 3$ (if it comes out as a fraction leave it like this, unless told otherwise)

4 Algebra is often used as a way of describing a rule, or formula, for finding the value of something (like the area of a circle, or volume of a pyramid). It can be used to solve problems. For example, think of a number, double it and add 12. If the result is, say, 20, we can denote the unknown number by n, and obtain

$$2n+12 = 20$$
$$2n+12-12 = 20-12$$
$$2n = 8$$
$$n = 4$$

So the number we started with was 4.

How to Do It

1 a Simplify the following:

    (i) $5a+3b+2a$

    (ii) $6c-3d+4d$

    (iii) $-3r+2s-5r-10s$

    (iv) $5b+3c-6b-4c+b$

    (v) $a^2 \times b^2 \times 2a^3$

    (vi) $7m^3n^2 \times 3m^4n^3$

    (vii) $15v^4w^3 \div 9v^3w^5$

    (viii) $14h^3k^3 \div 7hk^2$

Solution

    (i) $5a+3b+2a = 7a+3b$

    (ii) $6c-3d+4d = 6c+d$

    (iii) $-3r+2s-5r-10s = -8r-8s$

    (iv) $5b+3c-6b-4c+b = -c$

    (v) $a^2 \times b^2 \times 2a^3 = 2a^5b^2$

    (vi) $7m^3n^2 \times 3m^4n^3 = 21m^7n^5$

    (vii) $15v^4w^3 \div 9v^3w^5 = \dfrac{5v}{3w^2}$

    (viii) $14h^3k^3 \div 7hk^2 = 2h^2k$

> *'Formulae are just a shorter and easier way of putting over ideas which would be clumsy if written down in ordinary English'*

147

b Solve each of the following equations:

(i) $6m + 11 = 25 - m$ (ii) $\dfrac{m}{2} + \dfrac{m}{3} - 3 = 2 + \dfrac{m}{6}$

(iii) $\dfrac{3 - 2t}{4} = \dfrac{4 - 5t}{3}$

Solution

(i) $6m + 11 = 25 - m$

Add m and subtract 11 from both sides:

$6m + m = 25 - 11$

$7m = 14$

$m = 2$

(ii) $\dfrac{m}{2} + \dfrac{m}{3} - 3 = 2 + \dfrac{m}{6}$

Multiply both sides by 6:

$3m + 2m - 18 = 12 + m$

Rearrange – letters on one side, numbers on the other:

$4m = 30$

$m = 7.5$

(iii) $\dfrac{3 - 2t}{4} = \dfrac{4 - 5t}{3}$

Multiply both sides by 12:

$3(3 - 2t) = 4(4 - 5t)$

$9 - 6t = 16 - 20t$

$14t = 7$

$t = 0.5$

2 Solve the following equation:

$3(x - 1) - 4(2x + 3) = 20$

Solution

$$3(x-1)-4(2x+3) = 20$$

Remove the brackets first – careful with that minus sign!

$$3x-3-8x-12 = 20$$
$$-5x-15 = 20$$

Add 15 to both sides:

$$-5x = 35$$
$$x = -7$$

3 Rewrite each of the following formulae to make the given letter the subject:

(i) $a+b = s+t$ (t)   (ii) $x^2+y = z$ (x)   (iii) $a = \sqrt{\dfrac{b+c}{2b}}$ (b)

Solution

(i) $a+b = s+t$

Reverse the order:

$$s+t = a+b$$
$$t = a+b-s$$

(ii) $x^2+y = z$
$$x^2 = z-y$$
$$x = \sqrt{z-y}$$

(iii) $a = \sqrt{\dfrac{b+c}{2b}}$

Square both sides:

$$a^2 = \dfrac{b+c}{2b}$$

Multiply both sides by $2b$:

$$2a^2b = b+c$$
$$2a^2b-b = c$$
$$b(2a^2-1) = c$$

$$b = \dfrac{c}{(2a^2-1)}$$

4a The sum of four consecutive numbers is 98; what are the numbers?

Solution

Let n be the smallest of the numbers. The other numbers are $n+1$, $n+2$ and $n+3$. So

$$n+(n+1)+(n+2)+(n+3) = 98$$
$$4n+6 = 98$$
$$4n = 92$$
$$n = 23$$

So the numbers are 23, 24, 25 and 26.

‘Remember to convert your equation solution into an answer for the question’

b In a newsagent's, the *Daily Bugle* costs 10p more than the *Daily Planet*. During one week Samantha bought 3 copies of the *Daily Bugle* and 4 copies of the *Daily Planet*. The total cost was £2.75. How much does each of the papers cost?

Solution

Let the cost of the *Daily Planet* be x pence. The cost of the *Daily Bugle* is therefore $(x+10)$ pence. So

$$3(x+10)+4x = 275 \text{ pence}$$
$$3x+30+4x = 275$$
$$7x+30 = 275$$
$$7x = 245$$
$$x = 35$$

So the cost of the *Daily Planet* is 35p and the cost of the *Daily Bugle* is 45p.

Do It Yourself

1a Simplify:

(i) $2c-c+4c$ (ii) $4t \times 3t$ (iii) $x^9 \div x^4$
(iv) $-6x-3y+10x+5y$ (v) $5b+3c-4c-4b+c$
(vi) $7f+2g-3f+g$ (vii) $-3r+2s-5r-10s$

b If $a=3$, $b=2$, $c=1$ and $d=5$, find the value of:

(i) $5a+2b-c-d$ (ii) $\dfrac{a+2b+3c+4d}{abcd}$

(iii) $\sqrt{ad+c}$ (iv) $(b+2d)^2-a^2$

2a Simplify:

    (i) $(2t^2)^3 \div 4t$ (ii) $5(m+1)(m-1)$ (iii) $(4r-3)(5-2r)$

b Remove the brackets and simplify as far as possible:

    (i) $3(x-2)+4(x+8)$ (ii) $4(z-2)-7(z-5)$

    (iii) $2(a+3b)+3(4a+5b)$ (iv) $(p+2)(p-5)$

    (v) $(x+2)^2$ (vi) $(3y+2x)(7z-5w)$

3a Solve the following equations:

    (i) $\dfrac{3x-4}{5} = 4$

    (ii) $3-x = 6+2x$

    (iii) $6(x+1)+7 = -5$

    (iv) $3y+1 = 6+2y$

    (v) $5n+3 = 21-4n$

    (vi) $7t-2 = 30-t$

b Rearrange each of the following to make the given letter the subject of the formula:

    (i) $v = u+at$ (t)

    (ii) $a = p(m+n)$ (p)

    (iii) $p = x(L+b)$ (b) (*Hint:* first remove brackets)

    (iv) $c = \dfrac{v}{u+t}$ (u)

    (v) $t = 2\pi\sqrt{\dfrac{h}{g}}$ (h)

4 A rectangular hall is 4 metres wider than it is high, and it is 8 metres longer than it is wide. The total area of the walls is 512 m². Using x for the height of the hall in metres, write down expressions for:

    (i) the width of the hall

    (ii) the length of the hall

    (iii) the area of each of the walls

Form an equation and solve it to find the dimensions of the hall.

Answers

Section 1

1 a (i) 9300   9330   9326.69
    (ii) 100   85.5   85.51
    (iii) 200   227   227.25

  b (i) 2.65   (ii) 6.63   (iii) 0.556   (iv) 11.6

2

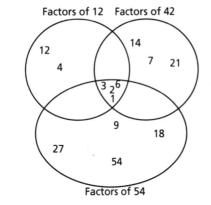

Factors of 12   Factors of 42

12, 4

14, 7, 21

3, 2, 6, 1

9, 18

27, 54

Factors of 54

3   101, 103, 107, 109, 113, 127, 131, 137, 139, 149

4   Multiples of 7   42, 70, 77, 84, 91
    Multiples of 11   33, 66, 77
    Multiples of 3   18, 33, 42, 51, 66, 84, 96
    25 has not been chosen.

5 a (i) 0.318 (3 s.f.)   (iii) 8
    (ii) 0.167 (3 s.f.)   (iv) 1.33 (3 s.f.)
    (v) 3 (on your calculator it may be just under 3)

  b (i) 0.75   (ii) 2.25   (iii) 3.08 (3 s.f.)

6   (i) -4 (ii) -14 (iii) 9
    (iv) -2 (v) 28   (vi) -7
    (vii) 50   (viii) 14   (ix) -240
    (x) $3\frac{3}{4}$ (or 3.75)

7   (i) 2^5 (ii) 4^7 (iii) 3^2 (iv) 2^6

8 a (i) 5.971×10^3 (ii) 7.8×10^4 (iii) 3.52×10^{-3}
    (iv) 1.4×10^7

  b (i) $n = 5$ (ii) 0.0041

  c (i) 1.5×10^{-2} (or 0.015)   (ii) 1.2×10^3 (or 1200)

Section 2

1   (i) 3   (ii) 10 and 15   (iii) 1 and 10

2 $35^2 = 30 \times 40 + 25 = 1225$
    $45^2 = 40 \times 50 + 25 = 2025$
    $55^2 = 50 \times 60 + 25 = 3025$
    $65^2 = 60 \times 70 + 25 = 4225$
    $75^2 = 70 \times 80 + 25 = 5625$
    $85^2 = 80 \times 90 + 25 = 7225$
    $95^2 = 90 \times 100 + 25 = 9025$

3   1, 8, 27, 64, 125, 216, 343, 512, 729, 1000
    64 is a square number (8^2) and 729 is a square number (27^2)
    The next number after 10 whose cube is also a square number is 16 ($16^3 = 4096$ and $4096 = 64^2$).

4 (i)

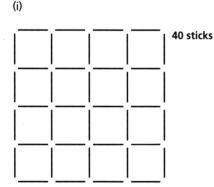

40 sticks

(ii) $4 \times 10 = 40$ and $5 \times 12 = 60$ – the answers seem to be the number of sticks required for each of the square patterns, with the first number of the multiplication indicating the number of squares along the side.

(iii) Using the number pattern in (ii) the number of sticks $= 6 \times 14 = 84$.

(iv) By extending the number patterns in (ii) we get $7 \times 16 = 112$, so it is the seventh square in the series.

5 **a** (i) 15 and 18 (they go up in 3s)
(ii) 16 and 19 (add on 3 to the previous term)
(iii) 20 and 25 (go up in 5s)
(iv) 8 and 5 (3 less than the term before)

b (i) 38 and 47.
(ii) The difference from one term to the next is going up in the counting numbers. The first difference is 2, the next is 3, the one after that is 4 and so on.

c The numerator appears to cancel to give a value equal to the number of numbers in the original numerator, while the denominator seems to give a value which is one more than the number of numbers in the original denominator. So

$$1+3+5+7+9+ \ldots +197+199$$

is 100 numbers. As is

$$2+4+6+ \ldots +200.$$

So the final numerator is 100 and the final denominator is 101, making the answer

$$\frac{100}{101}.$$

Section 3

1 (i) $\frac{3}{8}$ shaded, $\frac{5}{8}$ unshaded (ii) $\frac{4}{9}$ shaded, $\frac{5}{9}$ unshaded
(iii) $\frac{1}{2}$ shaded, $\frac{1}{2}$ unshaded (iv) $\frac{1}{2}$ shaded, $\frac{1}{2}$ unshaded

2 $\frac{1}{8}$ $\frac{1}{4}$ $\frac{5}{16}$ $\frac{3}{8}$ $\frac{7}{16}$ $\frac{1}{2}$ $\frac{9}{16}$ $\frac{5}{8}$ $\frac{11}{16}$ $\frac{3}{4}$ $\frac{7}{8}$

3 $\frac{3}{4}$ $\frac{1}{3}$ $\frac{3}{10}$ $\frac{2}{9}$ $\frac{2}{5}$ $\frac{1}{2}$

4 $\frac{18}{5}$ $3\frac{3}{5}$

5 $2\frac{3}{7} = \frac{17}{7}$
The smallest number of people is 7 and the smallest number of loaves is 17.

6 **a** (i) $\frac{13}{15}$ (ii) $\frac{17}{20}$ (iii) $\frac{16}{35}$
(iv) $\frac{5}{18}$

b £90.66

7 (i) 0.68 (ii) 7.417 (3 d.p.) (iii) 12.475

8 (i) $\frac{6}{11}$ (ii) $\frac{1}{9}$

Section 4

1 **a** (i) 0.9 (ii) 0.57 (iii) 0.205
(iv) 0.07 (v) 0.75 (vi) 0.6
(vii) 0.65 (viii) 0.975

b (i) $\frac{14}{25}$ (ii) $\frac{22}{25}$ (iii) $\frac{3}{25}$
(iv) $\frac{1}{20}$

2 (i) 0.27 (ii) 0.65 (iii) 0.4
(iv) 0.08

3 The percentages in original order are 62.5, 63.636 . . ., 65, 60, 50.
The fractions in order are $\frac{1}{2}, \frac{3}{5}, \frac{5}{8}, \frac{7}{11}, \frac{13}{20}$.

4 **a** £46.75

b £22.20 (to the nearest penny)

c (i) £233.83   (ii) £105.75   (iii) £37.01

d (i) Just under 8.5 cm (often taken to be 8.5 cm).
  (ii) Just under 5.5 cm (often taken to be 5.5 cm).
  (iii) 46.75 cm².
  (iv) As the quoted dimensions give an area of 40 cm²,
    the answer is 6.75 cm².
  (v) 16.875%.

e £4800

5 **a** (i) £18 : £27   (ii) 24 m : 18 m
  (iii) 14 kg : 21 kg : 28 kg

b 2.8 kg

c (i) 11.2 inches   (ii) 19 inches

Section 5

1 £23 700

2 Interest paid = £45
  interest rate per annum = 13.04% (2 d.p.)

3 **a** £96

b 5 years

4 Interest for simple interest = £150
  interest for compound interest = £132.40.
  Simple interest is the better investment by £17.60.

5 (i) £225
  (ii) £9000 (over 10 years £27 000 is paid back)

Section 6

1 Height = 3 m, floor area = 10.9375 m²,
  volume = 32.8125 m³

2 The answer by calculation is 283.56 m. By drawing, an
  answer of about 280 m is acceptable.

3 Distance = 252 m on a bearing of 308°

4 (i) Distance = 7.2 km on a bearing of 066°
  (ii) Distance = 18 km on a bearing of 357°

Section 7

1 **a** (i) 7.431 kg   (ii) 0.3761 kg   (iii) 4500 kg

b 34.5 kg

c 0.7 mg   700 mg   70 g   0.7 kg

d 650 g

e £29.70

f Weight = 6 g, thickness = 0.14 mm.

2 **a** (i) 46 mm   (ii) 79 mm   (iii) 9100 mm
  (iv) 31 200 mm

b (i) 500 cm   (ii) 920 cm   (iii) 74 cm
  (iv) 643.1 cm

c (i) 0.8 km   (ii) 0.004 km   (iii) 0.000 65 km
  (iv) 0.021 km

3 14.2 cl

Section 8

1 a (i) 168.7 cm (1 d.p.)   (ii) 169 cm   (iii) 162 cm

b (i) 2 goals   (ii) 1.5 goals   (iii) 0 goals

2

No. of words	1	2	3	4	5	6	7	8	9	10	11	12
Frequency	3	1	3	0	1	3	0	5	5	5	2	2

3 a

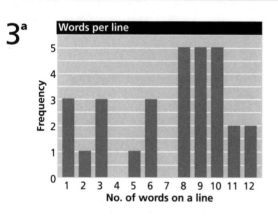

Words per line

b (i)

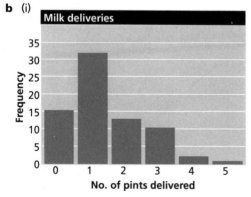

Milk deliveries

(ii) 73 houses
(iii) 32 houses received just one pint of milk.
(iv) 101 pints of milk were delivered.

4

Mark groups	1–5	6–10	11–15	16–20	21–25	26–30	31–35	36–40	41–45	46–50
Frequency	2	6	8	10	6	3	2	1	1	1

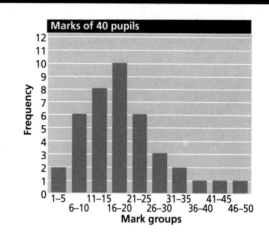

Marks of 40 pupils

The modal class is 16–20.

5 a

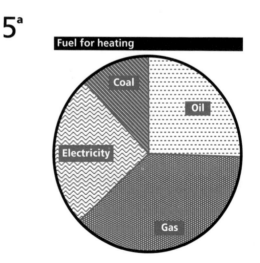

Fuel for heating

b UK – £2 700 000   Denmark – £1 800 000
Israel – £450 000   USA – £1 125 000
Germany – £2 025 000

c (Switzerland 126°, UK 108°, North America 72°, elsewhere 54°)

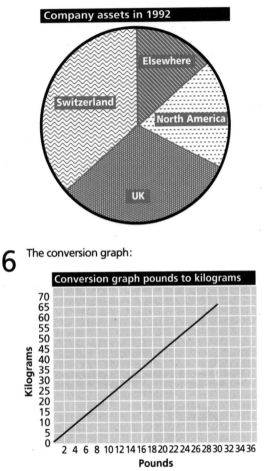

Company assets in 1992

6 The conversion graph:

Conversion graph pounds to kilograms

15 lb = 33 kg   8 kg = $3\frac{1}{2}$ lb

7

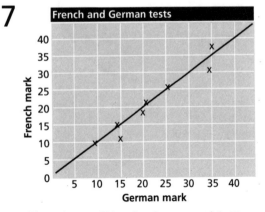

French and German tests

The estimate of his or her German mark is 17.

8 **a** (i) $\frac{5}{100}$ or $\frac{1}{20}$ or 0.05   (ii) $\frac{85}{99}$

b

	1	1	1	2	2	3
1	2	2	2	3	3	4
2	3	3	3	4	4	5
3	4	4	4	5	5	6
3	4	4	4	5	5	6
5	6	6	6	7	7	8
5	6	6	6	7	7	8

(i) $\frac{8}{36}$ or $\frac{2}{9}$
(ii) $\frac{7}{36}$
(iii) Trish – there are more ways of getting 4

9 **a**

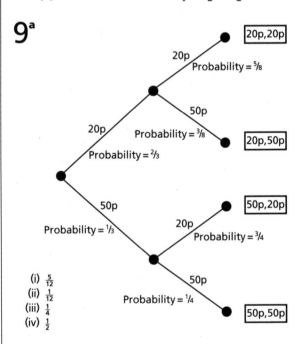

Probability = $\frac{2}{3}$
20p
Probability = $\frac{5}{8}$ → 20p,20p
50p
Probability = $\frac{3}{8}$ → 20p,50p

Probability = $\frac{1}{3}$
50p
Probability = $\frac{3}{4}$ → 50p,20p
50p
Probability = $\frac{1}{4}$ → 50p,50p

(i) $\frac{5}{12}$
(ii) $\frac{1}{12}$
(iii) $\frac{1}{4}$
(iv) $\frac{1}{2}$

b

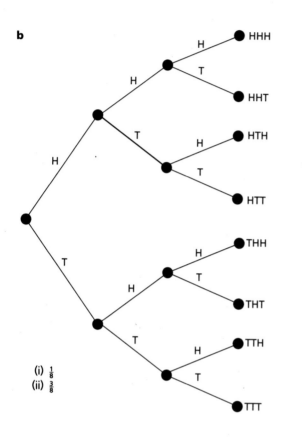

(i) $\frac{1}{8}$
(ii) $\frac{3}{8}$

Section 9

1

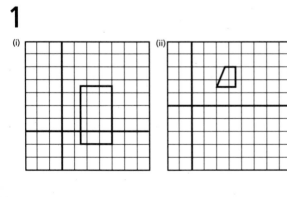

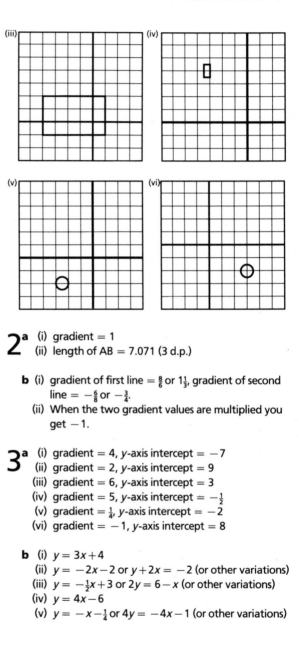

2ᵃ (i) gradient = 1
   (ii) length of AB = 7.071 (3 d.p.)

   b (i) gradient of first line = $\frac{8}{6}$ or $1\frac{1}{3}$, gradient of second
       line = $-\frac{6}{8}$ or $-\frac{3}{4}$.
       (ii) When the two gradient values are multiplied you
       get -1.

3ᵃ (i) gradient = 4, y-axis intercept = -7
   (ii) gradient = 2, y-axis intercept = 9
   (iii) gradient = 6, y-axis intercept = 3
   (iv) gradient = 5, y-axis intercept = $-\frac{1}{2}$
   (v) gradient = $\frac{1}{4}$, y-axis intercept = -2
   (vi) gradient = -1, y-axis intercept = 8

   b (i) $y = 3x + 4$
       (ii) $y = -2x - 2$ or $y + 2x = -2$ (or other variations)
       (iii) $y = -\frac{1}{2}x + 3$ or $2y = 6 - x$ (or other variations)
       (iv) $y = 4x - 6$
       (v) $y = -x - \frac{1}{4}$ or $4y = -4x - 1$ (or other variations)

4^a (i)

4^a (i)

x	−4	−3	−2	−1	0	1	2	3	4
$y = x^2$	16	9	4	1	0	1	4	9	16

(ii)

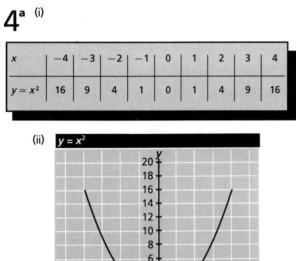

$y = x^2$

$1.8^2 = 3.2$, square root of $13 = \pm 3.6$

b

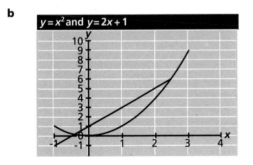

$y = x^2$ and $y = 2x + 1$

$x = 2.4$ or $−0.4$

c

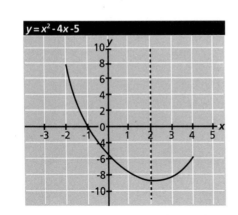

$y = x^2 - 4x - 5$

Section 10

1^a

1^a

Start time	Finish time	Length
08.00	08.40	0h 40m
14.15	15.25	1h 10m
16.50	17.40	0h 50m
19.30	21.00	1h 30m
11.40	14.05	2h 25m

b

Start time	Finish time	Length
8.00 a.m.	8.40 a.m.	0h 40m
2.15 p.m.	3.25 p.m.	1h 10m
4.50 p.m.	5.40 p.m.	0h 50m
7.30 p.m.	9.00 p.m.	1h 30m
11.40 a.m.	2.05 p.m.	2h 25m

2 **a** The coach arrives at 18.05. Average speed = 57.6 miles/hour.

b (i) 9.20 a.m. (ii) 40.5 miles/hour

c (i) 38 km (ii) $12\frac{2}{3}$ km/h

3 (i) 10 minutes (ii) 4 minutes (iii) 1000 m
(iv) 2000 m or 2 km

Section 11

1 $a = 132°$, $b = 65°$, $c = 42°$, $d = 83°$, $e = 55°$, $f = 60°$, $g = 45°$, $h = 120°$.

2a The ship is in danger for about 27 minutes (the length of path in danger is 4.47 miles).

b The curve looks like:

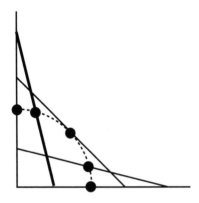

c A spiral like:

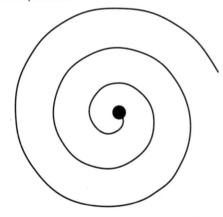

The horse can walk round the post five times.

Section 12

1 $a = 35°$, $b = 76°$

2 Just under 70°

3 $c = 115°$, $d = 65°$, $e = 65°$

4a (i) 36° (ii) 144°

b (i) 12 sides (ii) 150°

5a AC = 16.97 cm, AD = 20.78 cm

b (Joining the centres produces an isosceles triangle – height is 10.58 cm) height of pack = 20 cm, length of pack = 48 cm, width of pack = 26.58 cm

6a (i) $x = 34.8°$ (ii) $y = 26.6°$ (iii) $z = 49°$

b (i) $x = 3$ cm (ii) $y = 6.3$ cm (iii) $z = 14.1$ cm

c (Height of pole = 5.36 m (2 d.p.)) Angle of elevation = 1.8°

Section 13

1 (i) CENTRE (ii) RADIUS (iii) TANGENT
(iv) MINOR ARC (v) DIAMETER (vi) SECTOR

2a Distance = 8.64 cm

b Radius = 4.45 cm

c 31.4 m

d 11 210 mm² or 112.1 cm²

e 23 836 mm² or 238.4 cm² (or 238.3 cm² if you used pi = 3.14)

3a Each line is a tangent to the circle so from A to each of the points of contact is the same distance (call it a), similarly for all the other three points. So

$$AB = a+b \quad CD = c+d \quad BC = b+c \quad AD = a+d$$

Thus

$$AB + CD = a+b+c+d$$

and

$$BC + AD = b+c+a+d$$

b The angles are 54°, 56° and 70°.

Section 14

1 Eight shapes (including the one given), of which two have two lines of symmetry.

2

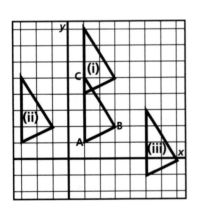

3a

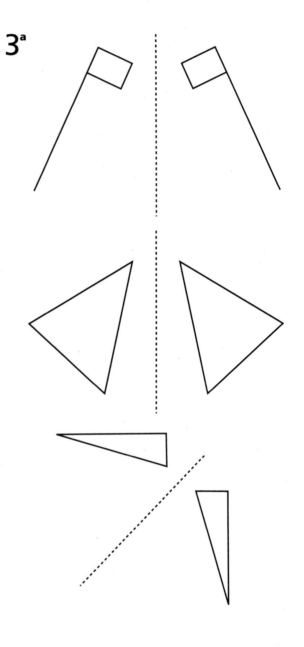

b

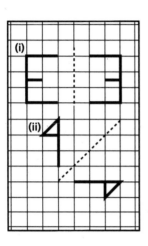

b

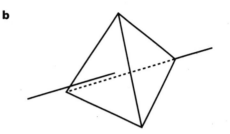

The diagram shows one of the axes of rotation – it is along the line joining a vertex to the middle of the opposite face and is at right angles to the face. There are three more such axes of rotation. Each of them has order 3.

4 a Three axes through the centre of the faces with rotational symmetry order 4

Six axes through centre of each edge to diagonally opposite edge with rotational order 2.

Four axes through diagonally opposite vertices with rotational symmetry order 3

5

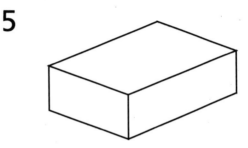

Opposite faces are congruent to each other.

6 a

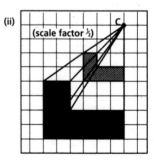

b 72 cm²

b

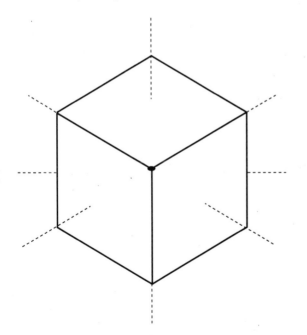

Section 15

1 Here is a net for each of them – there are others. If yours works, it is correct!

161

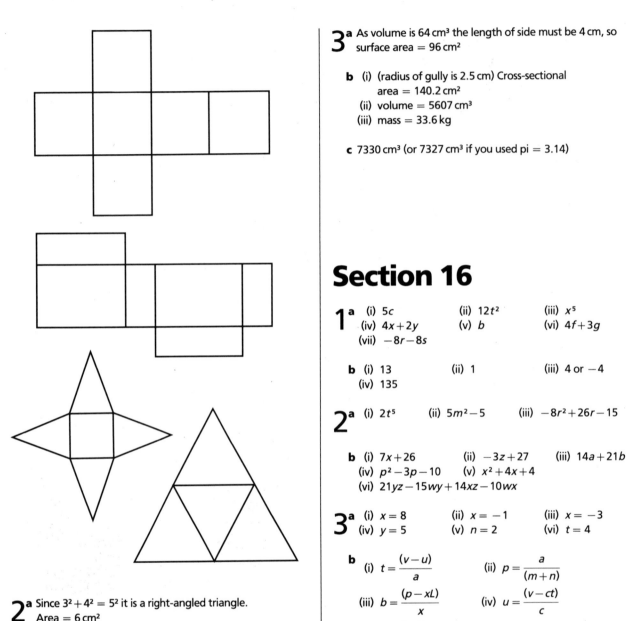

3 a As volume is 64 cm³ the length of side must be 4 cm, so surface area = 96 cm²

b (i) (radius of gully is 2.5 cm) Cross-sectional area = 140.2 cm²
(ii) volume = 5607 cm³
(iii) mass = 33.6 kg

c 7330 cm³ (or 7327 cm³ if you used pi = 3.14)

Section 16

1 a (i) $5c$ (ii) $12t^2$ (iii) x^5
(iv) $4x+2y$ (v) b (vi) $4f+3g$
(vii) $-8r-8s$

b (i) 13   (ii) 1   (iii) 4 or -4
(iv) 135

2 a (i) $2t^5$ (ii) $5m^2-5$ (iii) $-8r^2+26r-15$

b (i) $7x+26$ (ii) $-3z+27$ (iii) $14a+21b$
(iv) $p^2-3p-10$ (v) x^2+4x+4
(vi) $21yz-15wy+14xz-10wx$

3 a (i) $x=8$ (ii) $x=-1$ (iii) $x=-3$
(iv) $y=5$ (v) $n=2$ (vi) $t=4$

b (i) $t=\dfrac{(v-u)}{a}$ (ii) $p=\dfrac{a}{(m+n)}$

(iii) $b=\dfrac{(p-xL)}{x}$ (iv) $u=\dfrac{(v-ct)}{c}$

(v) $h=\dfrac{(gt^2)}{(4\pi^2)}$

4 (i) $x+4$ (ii) $x+12$ (iii) x^2+4x, x^2+12x
Equation is

$$2(x^2+14x)+2(x^2+12x)=512$$
$$x=8 \text{ or } -16 \ (-16 \text{ is silly for the height})$$

Dimensions are height = 8 m, width = 12 m, length = 20 m.

2 a Since $3^2+4^2=5^2$ it is a right-angled triangle.
Area = 6 cm²

b (i) perimeter = 16 cm
(ii) the unshaded area = 6.25 cm²
(iii) the shaded area = 9.75 cm²
(iv) the width of the band = 2.12 cm

c 67.36 cm² (An isosceles triangle is formed by the centre of the circle and the two points of contact of the circle's circumference with the table edge. Find the angle at the centre and then find the area of the triangle.)

Sample Exam Paper

1 (i) Express 48 as a product of prime numbers.
   (ii) Express 60 as a product of prime numbers.
  (iii) Use your answers to parts (i) and (ii) to find the smallest number that 48 and 60 divide into exactly.

2 Mr Kelly sells three different types of apples in his shop, Cox's, Worcesters and Granny Smiths, in the ratio 4 : 3 : 2. In a given week, he sold 216 lb of apples altogether. How many of each type did he sell?

    The cost and selling prices of the apples are given in the following table. How much profit did he make selling apples that week?

Type	Cox	Worcester	Granny Smith
Selling price per pound	60p	48p	65p
Cost price per pound	40p	30p	35p

3 The table shows part of a number pattern. A box has been drawn around four of the numbers. The marked box can be referred to as the '10' box.

```
 3    6    9    12

 7   10   13    16

11   14   17    20

15   18   21    24
```

(i) What is the sum of the numbers in the '26' box?

(ii) Write down in terms of n, the numbers that appear in the 'n' box.

(iii) (a) What is the sum of the numbers in the 'n' box? Simplify your answer.

(b) If this sum is 94, what is n?

4 John cycles $4\frac{1}{2}$ miles to school each day. He usually leaves home at 8.00 a.m. On the way, he has to go across a level crossing. On Monday, he reached the level crossing at 8.10 a.m. and had to wait for 3 minutes. He then cycled the rest of the journey at the same average speed as he had done for the first part. He arrived at school at 8.33 a.m.

(i) For how long was he cycling?

(ii) What average speed was he travelling at?

(iii) How far is the level crossing from his house?

(iv) Draw on graph or squared paper the travel graph for his journey.

5 Explain carefully why it is not possible to make a tile pattern that tessellates, using tiles that are in the shape of a regular pentagon.

6 Jasmine and Gabby belong to the local rowing club. They are looking at a course for a competition, and decided to make a scale drawing of it using a scale of 1 cm to 200 m. The course is as follows: Start at A, row 600 m on a bearing of 030 ° to B. Then row 800 m on a bearing of 100 ° to C. Then you row due south 400 m to D, before returning to A.

    (i) Make an accurate copy of their drawing.
    (ii) What is the total length of the course in metres?
    (iii) What bearing do they row on the final part from D to A?

7 If $p = -\frac{1}{4}$, and $q = 1\frac{1}{2}$, evaluate:

    (i) $4p + 6q$ (ii) $\dfrac{p+q}{p-q}$

8 The diagram shows a circle drawn inside a square so as to just touch in four places. If the perimeter of the circle is 20 cm, find the area shaded in the diagram.

9 The diagram shows a ladder AB of length 3.8 m resting against a vertical wall, standing on horizontal ground. Because of rubble lying on the ground, A cannot be put nearer than 0.8 m to the base of the wall N. The bottom of a window C is 5.2 m above N. With the ladder resting against the wall, calculate the smallest distance that BC could equal.
    In this position, what is the angle that the ladder makes with the ground?

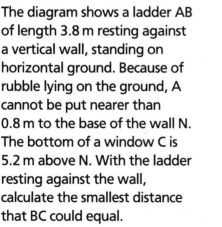

10 Calculate:

(i) $4^{-1/2}$ (ii) $3^3 \times 4^{-2} \times 5^0$

(iii) the square root of one thousand million, giving your answer in standard form correct to three significant figures.

11 Here are the first four rows of a number pattern.

Row 1   2   . . . .
Row 2   4 + 6   . . . .
Row 3   8 + 10   . . . .
Row 4   12 + 14   . . . .

(i) Find the sum of the numbers in each row.
(ii) Describe the numbers you obtain.
(iii) What is the sum of numbers in the 20th row?
(iv) If this pattern continues, what will be the sum of the numbers in the nth row?

12 A bag contains coloured discs, 3 red, 4 blue and 5 green. Two discs are taken from the bag, the first being replaced before the second is removed.

(i) Complete the following probability tree.

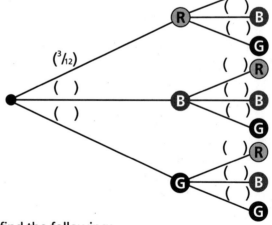

Use the tree to find the following:

(ii) the probability that both discs are red.
(iii) the probability that both discs are the same colour.
(iv) the probability that neither disc is green.

13 An atomic particle moves 4.83×10^{-1} metres in 8.64×10^{-6} seconds. Calculate the speed of the particle in centimetres/second, giving your answer in standard form correct to three significant figures.

14 Copy the diagram shown alongside.

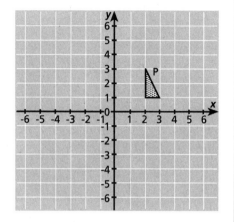

  (i) Reflect P in the line $x = 1.5$. Label the image Q.
  (ii) Rotate Q by 90° clockwise about the point $(0, -1)$. Label the image R.
  (iii) Reflect R in the line $x = 1.5$. Label it S.
  (iv) Describe the single transformation that will map S on to P.

15 The marks obtained by 80 pupils in a mathematics test are summarised in the table on the next page.

  (i) Copy and complete the table.
  (ii) Use the Frequency × Middle Value column to find an approximation to the mean score.
  (iii) Draw a cumulative frequency curve for these data on graph paper.
  (iv) Use your graph to find the interquartile range.

Mark	Frequency	Group middle value	Frequency × middle value	Cumulative frequency
1–10	2			
11–20	3			
21–30	4			
31–40	15			
41–50	25			
51–60	21			
61–70	6			
71–80	4			
Total				

Solutions

1
(i) $48 = 2 \times 24 = 2 \times 2 \times 12 = 2 \times 2 \times 2 \times 6$
$= 2 \times 2 \times 2 \times 2 \times 3$
(ii) Similarly, $60 = 2 \times 2 \times 3 \times 5$
(iii) The lowest common multiple is

$2 \times 2 \times 2 \times 2 \times 3 \times 5 = 240$

2
$4 + 3 + 2 = 9$ parts
$216 \div 9 = 24$, so 1 part $= 24$ lb
He sells: $4 \times 24 = 96$ lb of Cox's
$3 \times 24 = 72$ lb of Worcesters
$2 \times 24 = 48$ lb of Granny Smiths
Profit: on Cox's $= 20$p per pound
on Worcesters $= 18$p per pound
on Granny Smiths $= 30$p per pound
Total profit $= 96 \times 20 + 72 \times 18 + 48 \times 30$ pence
$= £46.56$

3
(i) $26 + 29 + 30 + 33 = 118$
(ii) $n, n+3, n+4, n+7$
(iii) (a) $n + n + 3 + n + 4 + n + 7 = 4n + 14$
(b) $4n + 14 = 94$
$\therefore \quad 4n = 80 \qquad n = 20$

4
(i) 30 minutes
(ii) $4\frac{1}{2}$ miles in 30 minutes $= 9$ miles/hr
(iii) In 10 minutes, distance travelled $=$
$9 \times \frac{1}{6} = 1.5$ miles.
The crossing is $1\frac{1}{2}$ miles from his home.
(iv)

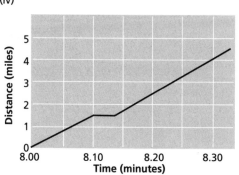

5

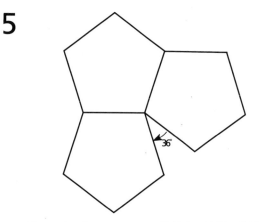

The angle of a pentagon $= 108°$. $3 \times 108° = 324°$,
which leaves a gap of $36°$ as shown.

6 (i)

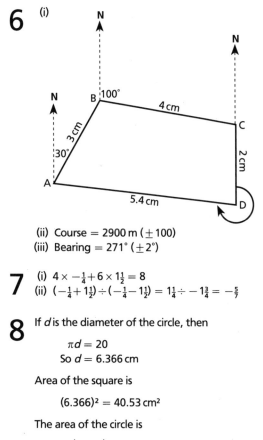

(ii) Course $= 2900$ m (± 100)
(iii) Bearing $= 271°$ ($\pm 2°$)

7
(i) $4 \times -\frac{1}{4} + 6 \times 1\frac{1}{2} = 8$
(ii) $(-\frac{1}{4} + 1\frac{1}{2}) \div (-\frac{1}{4} - 1\frac{1}{2}) = 1\frac{1}{4} \div -1\frac{3}{4} = -\frac{5}{7}$

8 If d is the diameter of the circle, then

$\pi d = 20$
So $d = 6.366$ cm

Area of the square is

$(6.366)^2 = 40.53$ cm²

The area of the circle is

$$\pi \left(\frac{6.366}{2}\right)^2 = 31.83 \text{ cm}^2$$

The shaded area is

$40.53 - 31.83 = 8.7$ cm²

9 $BN = \sqrt{3.8^2 - 0.8^2}$ (by Pythagoras)
$= 3.71\,\text{m}$

So $BC = 5.2 - 3.71 = 1.49\,\text{m}$

$\cos \angle NAB = \dfrac{0.8}{3.8}$ hence $\angle NAB = 77.8°$

10 (i) $\frac{1}{2}$ (ii) $27 \times \frac{1}{16} \times 1 = \frac{27}{16}$
(iii) $\sqrt{1\,000\,000\,000} = 31\,622.8 = 3.16 \times 10^4$

11 (i) 2, 10, 18, 26
(ii) They increase by 8 starting at 2.
(iii) This sequence can be represented by $8n - 6$.
(6 less than the multiple of 8)
Hence the sum of numbers in the 20th row is

$8 \times 20 - 6 = 154$

(iv) $8n - 6$

12 (i)

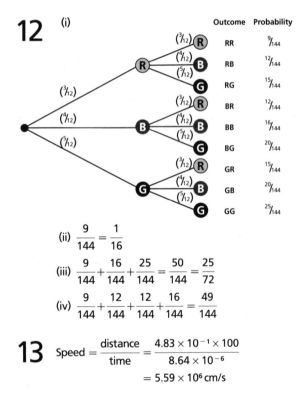

(ii) $\dfrac{9}{144} = \dfrac{1}{16}$

(iii) $\dfrac{9}{144} + \dfrac{16}{144} + \dfrac{25}{144} = \dfrac{50}{144} = \dfrac{25}{72}$

(iv) $\dfrac{9}{144} + \dfrac{12}{144} + \dfrac{12}{144} + \dfrac{16}{144} = \dfrac{49}{144}$

13 $\text{Speed} = \dfrac{\text{distance}}{\text{time}} = \dfrac{4.83 \times 10^{-1} \times 100}{8.64 \times 10^{-6}}$

$= 5.59 \times 10^6\,\text{cm/s}$

14 This question is best answered using tracing paper.
(i) (ii) (iii)

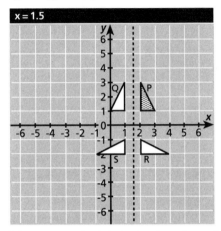

(iv) Rotation of 90° clockwise about $(3, -1)$

15 (i)

Mark	Frequency	Middle value (m)	$f \times m$	Cumulative frequency
1–10	2	5.5	11.0	2
11–20	3	15.5	46.5	5
21–30	4	25.5	102.0	9
31–40	15	35.5	532.5	24
41–50	25	45.5	1137.5	49
51–60	21	55.5	1165.5	70
61–70	6	65.5	393.0	76
71–80	4	75.5	302.0	80
Total	80		3690.0	

(ii) $3690 \div 80 = 46.1$

(iii)

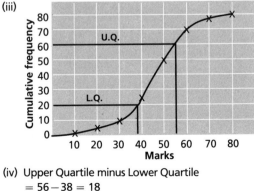

(iv) Upper Quartile minus Lower Quartile
$= 56 - 38 = 18$

Index

Titles in *The Way to Pass* series

These books are available at £7.99 each from all good bookshops or directly from Vermilion (post and packing free) using the form below, or on our credit card hotline on **0279 427203.**

ORDER FORM
National Curriculum Maths

				Quantity
Level 4	Key Stage 3	11-14 years	0 09 178116 7	....
Level 5	Key Stage 3	11-14 years	0 09 178118 3	....
Level 6	Key Stage 3	11-14 years	0 09 178125 6	....
GCSE Foundation Level	Key Stage 4	14-16 years	0 09 178123 X	....
GCSE Intermediate Level	Key Stage 4	14-16 years	0 09 178121 3	....
GCSE Higher Level	Key Stage 4	14-16 years	0 09 178127 2	....

National Curriculum English

Level 4	Key Stage 3	11-14 years	0 09 178129 9	....
Level 5	Key Stage 3	11-14 years	0 09 178135 3	....
Level 6	Key Stage 3	11-14 years	0 09 178133 7	....
GCSE	Key Stage 4	14-16 years	0 09 178131 0	....

Mr/Ms/Mrs/Miss...

Address:..

....

....

Postcode:.. Signed:..

HOW TO PAY
I enclose cheque / postal order for £......... : ....made payable to VERMILION
I wish to pay by Access / Visa card (delete where appropriate)

Card No ....Expiry date:...............................

Post order to **Murlyn Services Ltd, PO Box 50, Harlow, Essex CM17 ODZ.**

POSTAGE AND PACKING ARE FREE. Offer open in Great Britain including Northern Ireland. Books should arrive less than 28 days after we receive your order; they are subject to availability at time of ordering. If not entirely satisfied return in the same packaging and condition as received with a covering letter within 7 days. Vermilion books are available from all good booksellers

The Video Class Mathematics and *English* videos which accompany the above titles are available at £12.99 from leading video retailers and bookshops, or on the credit card hotline **0275 857017.**